Horsing Around in the Kitchen

Our most popular recipes,
Tested and requested hundreds of times,
By guests from all over the world

Ranch Recipes

BARRIER, CHAPARRAL
WESTERN VACATION RANCH

Kasandra
O'Bertos

Horsing Around in the Kitchen

by
Kasandra O'Bertos

First Printing – January 1997

Published by
Barrier Chaparral Western Vacation Ranch
P.O. Box 502
Tisdale, Saskatchewan
Canada   S0E 1T0

Canadian Cataloguing in Publication Data

O'Bertos, Kasandra, 1940 –

Horsing around in the kitchen

Includes index.
ISBN 1-895292-84-0

1. Cookery, Canadian – Prairie style.   2. Cookery –
Saskatchewan.   3. Ranch life – Saskatchewan – Humor.
I.   Barrier Chaparral Western Vacation Ranch.   II. Title.

TX715.6.026 1997   641.59'7124   C96-920174-5

Food Photography by: Patricia Holdsworth
Patricia Holdsworth Photography

All photographs taken at or near Barrier Chaparral Ranch

Cover and page design by: Brian Danchuk

Illustrations by: Kasandra O'Bertos, Ivan Allan, Trisha Olivier

Designed, Printed and Produced in Canada by:

Centax Books, a Division of PrintWest Communications Ltd.
Publishing Director, Photo Designer & Food Stylist: Margo Embury
1150 Eighth Avenue, Regina, Saskatchewan, Canada S4R 1C9
(306) 525-2304   FAX: (306) 757-2439

Table of Contents

Imagine sitting around a campfire beneath the wide open prairie sky . . . breathing in the rich aroma of barbecuing buffalo steaks, sourdough biscuits and freshly baked apple pie.

Now you can prepare not only these tempting cowboy classics in your own home on the range but also a wide variety of the Best of the West – from hearty chuckwagon cookouts to sizzling barbecues – from wild game and fish, to a potpourri of dishes that have made the Barrier Chaparral Vacation Ranch a culinary trail ride . . .

Recipes have been tested in U.S. Standard measurements. Common metric measurements are given as a convenience for those who are more familiar with metric. Recipes have not been tested in metric.

Howdy...

Horsing Around in the Kitchen – is exactly that. A cookbook with fun-to-make recipes and a lot of "horsing around". A few juicy tidbits of ranch-savvy humor and these wonderfully delicious and easy recipes will keep you entertained for years to come.

Running a "Dude Ranch" with a lot of Urban Cowboys makes for lots of laughter, and the adventure of riding the wide-open prairie and mysterious forest trails, ensures a hearty western appetite.

My affinity with nature and my love for horses and cooking, plus the fact that my husband, George, shares all these interests and is also an avid hunter, has led us to open Barrier Chaparral Vacation Ranch, in the beautiful province of Saskatchewan, Canada.

This book is the result of many years of entertaining and cooking for hundreds of guests from all over the world. This collection of new and old cooking ideas has been tested on our discriminating guests with enthusiastic feedback.

So, after being asked time and again, "Why don't you write a Ranch Cookbook?", I invested in a new typewriter instead of a new horse.

And I found that a well-trained horse and excellent riding habits are comparable to a good cookbook:
   Well balanced, adventurous and fun to do
   Easy to handle, rewarding
   No great expertise required, outdoorsy (see the photos)
   Sometimes exciting, sometimes relaxing; sometimes easy, sometimes challenging
   Sharpens the senses and lifts the spirit
   And always, always a "sweet" nuzzle at the end of a ride !!
   So here it is – to all friends of Good Food and Horses; from my hearth to yours!

After all, there is no love more sincere – than the love of food and horses. Enjoy.

My good friend Gloria Carriere cooked with me and contributed not just recipes, but also a tremendous amount of time and encouragement. Thank you, Gloria, for your good humor, good sense and support.

   With love,

   Kasandra

Kasandra O'Bertos

Introduction

Herbs & Spices

A dish without herbs and spices is a dish without sense.

The addition of herbs or spices to a dish enhances the subtle aroma of the food and not only sharpens the appetite but facilitates the digestion – as well as, of course, pleases the taste buds.

Basil: A stress-reducing, digestive aid, it goes well with fish, chicken and eggs, with peppers, eggplant and tomatoes.

Caraway Seeds: Used in Indian cooking (ajowan) and native medicine, caraway is also used as a seasoning in Central Europe. The seeds are used in sausages, cheeses, in rye and other breads, sauerkraut and fresh cabbage dishes and with meat, especially pork, and in some goulashes. Adding caraway seeds to bread doughs and soft cheese makes them both much more digestible.

Cloves: They strengthen and enrich flavors. Cloves are good with lamb, and onions cooked with cloves become sweeter.

Coriander: It lends superb flavor to mushroom dishes, meatballs, lamb stews or pork kabobs.

Ginger: A warming stimulant and an aid for digestion and digestive problems, ginger stimulates the gastric juices, which in turn facilitates good digestion.

Horseradish: More pungent than the strongest onion, horseradish is very good with eggs, chicken, roast beef, sausages and smoked fish.

Juniper Berries: Always associated with game, juniper berries can be cooked with game or used in stuffing. Use the berries in marinades for any game, or in sauerkraut. The berries were a food source of the North American Indians of the Pacific Northwest. They ground them to make into cakes and made tea from the stems and leaves.

Herbs & Spices

Marjoram: One of the most important culinary herbs, the ancient Egyptians used marjoram to enhance the flavor of meat and help assimilate the minerals from it. Always add it toward the end of the cooking time. It will help the digestion of vegetables like cabbage, beans and salads.

Nutmeg: Used in moderation, nutmeg enlivens food. Best for spicing egg dishes, sauces (a white or cheese sauce for cauliflower) and cakes, it goes particularly well with onions and spinach; mashed potatoes benefit from a good sprinkling.

Oregano: From the same family as marjoram but more pungent, oregano is very important in Italian cooking. Always cook mushrooms with marjoram and oregano, as all fungi contains a substance called chiten that can be very indigestible. Similarly, use both herbs when cooking cabbage, legumes and turnips, which can be equally indigestible and cause flatulence.

Pepper: The most widely used spice in the kitchen, pepper should always be bought whole and freshly ground in a mill, as it quickly loses its aroma when ground. Pepper should always be added at the last moment for the same reason. Coarsely ground black pepper has a delicious affinity with fresh strawberries.

Rosemary: It goes well with poultry, rabbit and lamb. Because of its antibacterial properties protects against possible putrefaction and helps digestion of the fat. Burn a few sprigs on the coals while barbecuing meat.

Thyme: A major cooking herb, the fragrance of thyme is long lasting, so it is good for long-cooking stews and casseroles. Thyme fixes the iron in meat, so it helps the digestion of stews and casseroles. Thyme is excellent for flavoring marinades, stuffings and soup stocks.

Rise & Shine

(Breakfasts)

Cowboy Coffee

This is the way the coffee was made at roundups for 100 years and still is to this day, on the trail over an open fire, or in the campground on a grill. It's a nectar for weary cowboys!!

You will need a large fireproof coffee pot.

5 gallons	cold water	22.5 L
5 cups	ground coffee	1.25 L
½ tsp.	salt	2 mL

1. Bring water to a rolling boil. Remove from heat and add coffee.
2. Lower the heat. Place the coffee back on the heat until the grounds submerge; DO NOT BOIL.

Pictured on page 51.

Coffee was the universal drink in the OLD WEST–

Grounds were left in the pot to be boiled and reboiled again and again.

It was jokingly said that coffee, it was also called "whistleberries", was not sufficiently strong unless you could float a silver dollar on it.

It had to be: Black as the Devil,
Strong as death,
Sweet as love, and
Hot as hell!!!

Basic Pancakes

1½ cups	flour	375 mL
2 tsp.	baking powder	10 mL
½ tsp.	salt	2 mL
3 tbsp.	sugar	45 mL
1	egg	1
1¼ cups	milk	300 mL
3 tbsp.	melted butter	45 mL

1. Sift flour before measuring. Measure and sift together all dry ingredients.
2. Beat the egg, and add milk and butter. Stir liquid into dry ingredients slowly.
3. Heat heavy frying pan. Pour batter from a pitcher or measuring cup to get even-shaped cakes. Cook pancakes until golden brown, turning once.

Yields: 6-7 pancakes

Variation: For Apple Pancakes, grate a peeled apple into batter. Add ¼ tsp. (1 mL) cinnamon.

Buttermilk Pancakes

1 cup	flour	250 mL
2 tsp.	baking powder	10 mL
¼ tsp.	salt	1 mL
3 tbsp.	sugar	45 mL
1	egg	1
1 cup	buttermilk	250 mL
3 tbsp.	melted butter	45 mL

1. Sift flour, before measuring. Measure and sift together all dry ingredients.
2. Beat the egg, then add buttermilk and butter. Stir liquid slowly into dry ingredients .
3. Heat heavy frying pan. Pour batter from a pitcher or measuring cup to get even-shaped cakes. Cook pancakes until golden brown, turning once.

Yields: 6-7, 5" (13 cm) pancakes

Variation: For Apple Buttermilk Pancakes, grate a peeled apple into batter. Add ¼ tsp. (1 mL) cinnamon.

Quark Pancakes

A very special breakfast treat for a very special day!

1 cup	quark*	250 mL
½ cup	half and half cream	125 mL
1 tsp.	vanilla	5 mL
¼ cup	sugar	60 mL
¼ tsp.	salt	1 mL
2	eggs, slightly beaten	2
1 cup	all-purpose flour	250 mL
1 tsp.	fast-rising yeast**	5 mL
	oil for frying	

1. Cream quark with the cream, vanilla, sugar, salt and eggs.
2. Add flour and yeast, mix well. Let rise 1 hour.
3. Pour batter into a hot oiled pan to form small pancakes; fry over medium heat until golden brown, turning once.

Yields: 8 servings.

Serve with Orange-Kiwi Sauce, page 89, or any fruit syrup

* Quark has a creamy soft texture; both flavor and texture are between cream cheese and cottage cheese. Instead of the quark you may use the same amount of cottage cheese creamed in a blender with half and half cream.

** For a simpler and faster version, substitute ½ tsp. (2 mL) baking powder for the yeast. Batter is ready to use in 10 minutes.

Pictured on page 17.

Baked Apple Pancake

1 tbsp.	butter	15 mL
4	medium apples, peeled and grated	4
3 tbsp.	lemon juice	45 mL
6	eggs	6
3 cups	all-purpose flour	750 mL
2 cups	milk	500 mL
1 tsp.	salt	5 mL
½ cup	sugar	125 mL
¼ cup	sliced almonds	60 mL
1 tsp.	cinnamon	5 mL

Baked Apple Pancake continued

1. Preheat oven to 375°F (190°C).
2. Butter a 9 x 13" (23 x 33 cm) baking pan generously.
3. Distribute apples evenly over butter in pan. Sprinkle with lemon juice.
4. In a large bowl or pitcher combine eggs, flour, milk and salt. Beat with electric mixer for 1 minute.
5. Pour batter over apples. Combine sugar, almonds and cinnamon; sprinkle over batter.
6. Bake for 40 minutes, or until puffed and golden brown.

Yields: 8-10 servings

Serve with your favorite pancake syrup.

Bucking Bronco Pancakes

Hold on to your saddle horn, folks! You never tasted pancakes quite like these.

1 cup	buckwheat flour	250 mL
1 cup	all-purpose flour	250 mL
2 tsp.	baking powder	10 mL
1 tsp.	baking soda	5 mL
1 tbsp.	sugar	15 mL
½ tsp.	salt	2 mL
2	eggs, lightly beaten	2
1 cup	milk	250 mL
½ cup	finely chopped walnuts	125 mL
2	large bananas, diced	2
1 tbsp.	vegetable oil	15 mL

1. Sift flours before measuring. Measure and sift together flours, baking powder and baking soda into a large bowl. Add sugar and salt.
2. Combine eggs and milk; add to flour mixture and stir just enough to combine. Stir in walnuts and bananas.
3. Heat pan or griddle, grease lightly with oil. Pour a small amount of batter onto griddle and cook until nicely browned, turning once.

Yields: 10-12 servings

Serve with maple syrup.

Trapper's Crispy Rice Pancakes

Here is a novel idea for leftover cooked rice. If you do not have leftovers, for your next rice meal make twice as much as you need and use the extra for these wonderfully delicious rice pancakes. Children love them for breakfast, lunch or in between.

2 cups	cooked rice, white OR brown	500 mL
1	small onion, chopped	1
3	eggs, beaten until frothy	3
2 tbsp.	Parmesan cheese	30 mL
½ tsp.	thyme	2 mL
	salt and pepper to taste	
⅓ cup	bread crumbs, OR enough to make ingredients stick together	75 mL
	oil for frying	

1. Mix all ingredients together; using your hands, blend well.
2. Cooked rice may vary in moisture content, so use enough bread crumbs to make pancake mixture solid enough to form small pancake patties.
3. Using your hands, form small 4" (10 cm) pancake patties, flatten to about ½" (1.3 cm) thickness.
4. Heat griddle or frying pan to fairly high heat. Grease lightly with oil and brown pancakes on each side until very crispy.

Yields: 4 servings

   Serve with coleslaw or carrot salad for a lunch treat.

Hint: This dish is ideal on the trail, at cook outs, or camping. You may also like to try the sweeter version, on the next page.

Sweet Trapper's Crispy Rice Pancakes

This sweet version can easily be made into an exciting dessert. Pour Kiwi-Orange Sauce, page 89, over it, and YOU are riding HIGH!!

2 cups	cooked, rice, white OR brown	500 mL
3	eggs, beaten frothy	3
2 tsp.	sugar	10 mL
½ tsp.	cinnamon	2 mL
⅓ cup	bread crumbs, OR enough to make ingredients stick together	75 mL

1. Mix all ingredients together; using your hands; blend well.
2. Cooked rice may vary in moisture content, so use enough bread crumbs to make pancake mixture solid enough to be able to form small pancake patties.
3. Using your hands, form small 4" (10 cm) pancake patties, flatten to ½" (1.3 cm) thickness.
4. Heat griddle or frying pan to fairly high heat. Grease lightly with oil and brown pancakes on each side until very crispy.

Yields: 4 servings

   Serve with maple or fruit syrup.

Rise & Shine

Oven French Toast

A special favorite at the ranch! A breakfast where you all can sit down and eat hot French toast at the same time. This is perfect for a large group and the syrup is included.

12 oz.	loaf French bread, cut in thick slices	340 g
8	large eggs	8
1 cup	milk	250 mL
1 cup	cream	250 mL
2 tsp.	vanilla	10 mL
½ tsp.	nutmeg	2 mL
½ tsp.	cinnamon	2 mL
½ tsp.	mace	2 mL

Caramel Topping:

½ cup	butter, softened	125 mL
1 cup	brown sugar	250 mL
3 tbsp.	dark corn syrup	45 mL
1¼ cups	coarsely chopped pecans, walnuts OR hickory nuts*	300 mL

1. Heavily butter a 9 x 13" (23 x 33 cm) pan.
2. Layer pan with bread slices to within ½" (1.3 cm) of the top. Set aside.
3. In a blender mix eggs, milk, cream, vanilla, nutmeg, cinnamon and mace.
4. Pour egg mixture over bread slices. Refrigerate, covered, overnight.
5. Make topping by combining all topping ingredients. Set aside until time to bake French toast. Spread topping over bread.
6. Bake at 350°F (180°C) for 50 minutes, or until puffy and golden. Shield top with foil if it browns too quickly.

Yields: 8-10 servings

* Nuts may be omitted if you prefer. Raisins may be substituted for nuts. Sprinkle raisins between bread layers and on top.

Prairie Wheat Treat

From the wheat capital of the world to you . . . this may be served for breakfast, dessert, as a complement to any meal or as a snack!

1½ cups	whole wheat kernels	375 mL
8 oz.	quark*	250 mL
14 oz.	can crushed pineapple	398 mL
2 tbsp.	lemon juice	30 mL
6 oz.	pkg. instant vanilla pudding	170 g
2 cups	non-dairy whipped topping	500 mL

1. Soak wheat in lots of water for 4-5 hours.
2. Place in a slow cooker**. Cover with water and cook over low heat for 5-6 hours. DO NOT BOIL. Keep adding water as needed.
3. Drain wheat, rinse and cool.
4. Mix together creamed quark, crushed pineapple and lemon juice.
5. Add box of pudding (just as it comes). Add wheat and mix. Add the whipped topping and mix before serving.
6. Keeps well in the refrigerator for 2-3 days, or better still, freeze it!

Yields: 8-10 servings

Optional: * You can substitute creamed cottage cheese blended until smooth.
         ** Wheat may be cooked in a slow oven overnight at 200°F (100°C) or on the top of the stove on low heat for 1½-2 hours, stirring often.

Honeyed Barley Yogurt

Here is a breakfast, lunch or snack for the health or diet conscious!

2 tsp.	honey	10 mL
1 cup	plain yogurt	250 mL
1½ cups	cooked barley	375 mL
1 tsp.	vanilla	5 mL
	pinch of nutmeg	

1. Heat the honey in a microwave oven on HIGH for ½ minute.
2. Stir all ingredients together and chill.

Yields: 4-5 servings

Amigos Wake-Me-Ups

An unusual and spicy breakfast – Mexican food lovers can't get enough! Go easy on the chilies if you like it less hot.

8	corn tortillas OR 2 cups (500 mL) broken tortilla chips	8
5	slices bacon, diced	5
⅓ cup	chopped green onions	75 mL
1	jalapeño chili, minced	1
8	eggs, lightly beaten	8
	salt and pepper to taste	

1. Cut each corn tortillas into 8 wedges.
2. In a large skillet, fry bacon until cooked but not crisp. Add onions and chile, sauté. Add tortillas and cook until wedges are soft.
3. Pour eggs over tortillas and cook. Season with salt and pepper. Stir gently until firm or to your taste.

Yields: 4-6 servings

   Serve with medium or hot chunky salsa and extra tortilla chips.

Pictured opposite.

Rise & Shine (Breakfast)

Amigos Wake-Me-Ups with
   Chunky Salsa, page 16

Quark Pancakes, page 10

Orange-Kiwi Sauce, page 89

Homesteader's Oatmeal Bread, page 27

A Very Special Rhubarb Jam, page 90

One-Eyed Buffaloes

Eggs and toast, plus a colorful tomato accompaniment, here is a one-pan breakfast. Children are fascinated by this breakfast and it's easy for them to eat.

2 tbsp.	butter OR margarine	30 mL
8 slices	white, whole-wheat OR cheese bread	8 slices
8	eggs	8
	salt and pepper to taste	
8	tomato slices	8
1 tbsp.	diced green onions	15 mL

1. Spread butter or margarine on both sides of the bread.
2. With a 3" (7 cm) cookie cutter remove the center of each bread slice.
3. Place bread slices in medium hot pan, and very gently slide an egg into the "eye" of each slice. Cook half way through and turn; sprinkle with salt and pepper.
4. Brown the cut-out rounds along side the one-eyed buffaloes, place tomato slices on them and sprinkle with salt, pepper and onions. Serve with the Buffaloes.

Yields: 4-8 servings

Ranch-Style Eggs & Bacon

This recipe may be doubled or tripled easily. It's ideal for a large crowd.

2	slices bacon, diced	2
1	small onion, diced	1
⅓ cup	diced red peppers	75 mL
½ cup	sliced fresh mushrooms	125 mL
8	eggs	8
⅓ cup	shredded Cheddar cheese	75 mL
1 tsp.	chopped fresh dillweed	5 mL
	salt and pepper to taste	

1. Brown diced bacon until cooked, but not crisp.
2. Add onion, red peppers and mushrooms; sauté for 5 minutes.
3. Whip eggs until frothy; pour into pan. Sprinkle cheeses and dill on top.
4. Cook over medium heat, stirring, until eggs are thickened but still very moist. Salt and pepper to taste.

Yields: 6 servings

Serve with fried bacon and hash browns.

Barrier Chaparral Ranch, dining and quest cabins and a happy cowboy

Rise & Shine

Hash Brown Omelette

Bacon and eggs combined with hash browns and cheese make a great one-dish breakfast or lunch.

5	slices bacon	5
3 cups	frozen hash brown potatoes	750 mL
½ cup	chopped green pepper	125 mL
⅓ cup	zesty onion relish	75 mL
6	eggs	6
¼ cup	milk	60 mL
	salt and pepper to taste	
1 cup	shredded Cheddar cheese	250 mL

1. Cook bacon in a 10" (25 cm) frying pan until crisp. Remove from pan. Drain and dice.
2. Leave 2 tbsp. (30 mL) drippings in pan.
3. Add potatoes. Cook, stirring occasionally, until heated through.
4. Add green pepper and relish. Cook 15-20 minutes, or until underside is starting to crisp and brown.
5. Beat eggs, milk, salt and pepper together. Stir in cheese and bacon.
6. Pour eggs evenly over potatoes. Mix very lightly to let egg mixture seep through potatoes.
7. Cover, cook on low heat 8-10 minutes, or until eggs are set and cheese is melted. If desired, broil lightly to brown. Loosen edges; serve in wedges.

Yields: 4-6 servings

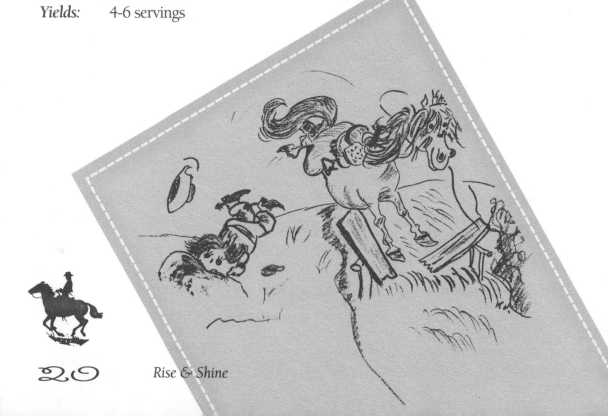

Western Brunch

Versatile and flavorful, this brunch favorite uses leftover barbecued chicken, steak, pork or even sausages.

1 tbsp.	butter OR vegetable oil	15 mL
12	slices bread	12
1-2 cups	thinly sliced leftover cooked meat	250-500 mL
4-6	green onions, chopped	4-6
2 cups	shredded cheese	500 mL
8	eggs	8
3 cups	milk	750 mL
1 tsp.	hot pepper sauce	5 mL
	salt and pepper to taste	

1. Grease a 9 x 13" (23 x 33 cm) baking dish with butter or oil.
2. Line the dish with half the bread slices. Top bread with half the meat, half the green onions and half the cheese.
3. Top with a second layer of bread. Add remaining meat, cheese and green onions.
4. Mix together eggs, milk and seasonings. Pour carefully over entire pan surface.
5. Cover and refrigerate 30 minutes or overnight.
6. Bake at 375°F (190°C) for 35-45 minutes, or until crisp, puffed and golden brown.

Yields: 8-10 servings

Quick-Draw Breakfast Dish

So called because the work is done the night before, this is fast, easy and delicious.

6 cups	bread cubes	1.5 L
1½ cups	½" (1.3 cm) ham cubes	375 mL
¼ cup	chopped green onions	60 mL
1½ cups	shredded Cheddar cheese	375 mL
6	eggs, beaten	6
1½ cups	buttermilk	375 mL
½ tsp.	salt	2 mL
¼ tsp.	pepper	1 mL
1	small garlic clove, minced	1

1. Grease a 9 x 13" (23 x 33 cm) pan generously. Place half the bread cubes in the pan. Scatter ham, onions and cheese over the bread. Cover with the remainder of the bread cubes.
2. Beat eggs until frothy, add buttermilk, salt, pepper and garlic salt; blend well. Pour evenly over bread cubes and refrigerate overnight.
3. Bake, uncovered, at 300°F (150°C) for 1-1½ hours. Cover top with foil if it browns too quickly.

Yields: 8-10 servings

Serve with toasted rye bread.

Roundup Breakfast

At roundup time there are always a lot of extra mouths to feed, so here is a real "crowd pleaser". This recipe gives you 15 servings, and preparation time is about 10-15 minutes.

2 tbsp.	butter	30 mL
18	eggs	18
1 cup	milk	250 mL
1 cup	sour cream	250 mL
½ cup	chopped green onions	125 mL
2 tbsp.	chopped fresh dill OR	30 mL
	1 tbsp. (15 mL) dried dillweed	
1 cup	finely chopped ham	250 mL
1 tsp.	salt	5 mL
½ tsp.	freshly ground pepper	2 mL

1. Preheat oven to 325°F (160°C).
2. Place butter in a 9 x 13" (23 x 33 cm) baking dish and melt in the oven. Tilt pan to coat bottom and sides.
3. Beat the eggs until smooth.
4. Whisk the milk into the sour cream; pour into eggs, beating until smooth.
5. Stir in onion, dill, ham, salt and pepper.
6. Pour into prepared dish and bake 35 minutes, or until puffed around the edges, set in center and tinged with brown.
7. Cut into squares and serve.

Yields: 15 servings

Serve with toast and bacon or sausage.

Rise & Shine

23

Mini Quiche Lorraine on Toasted English Muffins

3	eggs	3
1 cup	milk	250 mL
¼ tsp.	salt	1 mL
¼ tsp.	paprika	1 mL
	pinch of nutmeg	
2	green onions, sliced	2
¼ cup	grated Parmesan cheese	60 mL
¾ cup	grated Swiss cheese	175 mL
⅓ cup	chopped, cooked bacon, ham OR chicken	75 mL
3	English muffins	3

1. Butter 6 custard cups. Whisk eggs with milk, salt, paprika and nutmeg. Thinly slice green onions. Sprinkle onions, cheeses, and meat in bottoms of cups.
2. Pour in egg mixture.
3. Place cups in microwave, in a circle with space between each. Microwave, uncovered on high for 4 minutes.
4. Stir egg and move cooked edges to center. Microwave, uncovered, for 4 more minutes.
5. Let quiche stand for 5 minutes, then loosen edges and turn out onto toasted English muffins, or onto thick slices of ripe tomatoes.

Yields: 6 small quiche

Serve with fries or nachos.

Ranch Breads & Buns

Homemade Breads

Most of us remember the bread grandmother used to bake in her cozy kitchen. Fragrant, golden loaves – crusty, tender and delicious. Home bread making is not as common today and that is a pity because it is such a pleasant task and surprisingly easy.

The fabrication of commercial bread seems to have gone astray. Good-tasting healthy bread and buns are hard to find at our local supermarket and the cost is high.

No time? Well, the actual time for mixing bread dough is only 20 minutes. And it has an often overlooked psychological benefit – while you knead, slap and punch around that dough, you can get rid of all your bottled-up frustrations!

Try and Enjoy!

Today's Grandma

The old rocking chair will be empty today,
for grandma is no longer in it . . .

She's off in her car to her office or shop,
and buzzes around every minute . . .

No one can put grandma on a shelf,
she's versatile, forceful, dynamic!!

That isn't pie in the oven, you know,
her baking today is ceramic . . .

You won't see her trundling off early to bed,
from her place by a warm chimney nook . . .

Her typewriter clickety clacks through the night,
for grandma is writing a book . . .

Our heroine never allows backward looks,
to slow up her steady advancing . . .

She can't tend the babies anymore,
for grandma has taken up dancing . . .

She isn't content with crumbs of old thoughts,
with meager and secondhand knowledge,

So don't bring your mending for grandma to do,
for grandma's gone back to college!!

Homesteader's Oatmeal Bread

A sweet and moist breakfast bread, this is very tasty when toasted.

2 cups	water	500 mL
1 cup	rolled oats	250 mL
½ cup	molasses	125 mL
½ cup	cold water	125 mL
2 tbsp.	butter OR margarine	30 mL
1½ tsp.	salt	7 mL
1 cup	warm water	250 mL
2 tbsp.	yeast	30 mL
1 tsp.	sugar	5 mL
6-7 cups	all-purpose flour, approximately	1.5-1.75 L
	melted butter	

1. Combine water and rolled oats and cook for 2 minutes.
2. Add the next 4 ingredients to the oat mixture. Set aside until lukewarm.
3. Mix the warm water, yeast and sugar and let rise.
4. Combine both mixtures with enough all-purpose flour to make a dough that is smooth and not sticky after 10 minutes of kneading.
5. Place dough in a large greased bowl; grease top of dough and cover to prevent drying. Put in a warm place and let rise until doubled in bulk, 2 to 2½ hours.
6. Punch down the risen dough; let rest 10 minutes. Preheat oven to 350°F (180°C).
7. Form dough into 2 loaves and place in greased 5 x 9" (13 x 23 cm) bread pans. Let rise 1 hour.
8. Bake in a preheated oven for 1 hour.
9. Brush baked loaves with melted butter.

Yields: 2 loaves

Variation: You may add raisins or chopped walnuts or pecans to the bread.

Pictured on page 17.

Mrs. Lindsay's Pioneer Buns

This recipe was given to my husband 30 years ago by an old hunting friend, a real old-west character, whose wife supplied the whole moose-hunting party with these delicious buns for many years. So here is the most "fool-proof" bun recipe you will ever find.

1 cup	lukewarm water	250 mL
2 tbsp.	yeast	30 mL
1 tsp.	sugar	5 mL
2 cups	hot water	500 mL
½ cup	lard	125 mL
¾ cup	sugar	175 mL
2 cups	oat bran, softened with ¾ cup (175 mL) boiling water	500 mL
1½ cups	whole-wheat flour	375 mL
3	eggs	3
5 cups	all-purpose flour, approximately	1.25 L

1. Combine the first 3 ingredients and let rise until bubbly.
2. Combine the next 5 ingredients in order in a large bowl. Use an electric mixer to make a "liquid paste". Add more flour if mixture is too thin, add risen yeast and blend well.
3. Work in enough flour to form a soft dough. Knead 10 minutes until smooth and satiny. Place dough in a large greased bowl; grease top of dough and cover to prevent drying. Put in a warm place. Let rise until doubled in bulk, 1½ to 2 hours.
4. Punch down the risen dough; let rest 10 minutes.
5. Shape into desired roll or bun shapes and arrange on greased baking sheets, ½" (1 cm) apart. Cover and let rise until doubled in bulk, about 45 minutes.
6. Bake in preheated 375°F (190°C) oven for 20-25 minutes.
7. Brush baked buns with melted butter.

Variation: Brush the buns before baking with a glaze, to give them a brown shiny surface.

Yields: 30-40 buns, depending on the size

Egg Glaze:

1	egg white, slightly beaten	1
1 tbsp.	cold water	15 mL

Beat egg white and water together.

Quick Buns

1 tbsp.	yeast	15 mL
1 tsp.	sugar	5 mL
½ cup	lukewarm water	125 mL
1 cup	boiling water	250 mL
1 cup	cold water	250 mL
½ cup	sugar	125 mL
3 tbsp.	vegetable oil	45 mL
1½ tsp.	salt	7 mL
3	eggs	3
5-6 cups	all-purpose flour	1.25-1.5 L

1. Dissolve the yeast and sugar in the lukewarm water; let rise for 10 minutes.
2. Combine the boiling water and cold water and pour over the ½ cup (125 mL) sugar, oil and salt in a large bowl. Let stand while yeast is rising.
3. Beat the eggs; add to water mixture. Add the yeast mixture. Add 3 cups (750 mL) of flour and beat well. Add enough of the remaining flour to make a stiff dough.
4. Place dough in a large greased bowl; grease top of dough and put in a warm place; cover and let rise, punching down every 15 minutes for the first hour.
5. After an hour, punch down dough; shape into buns; put into greased pans and let rise for 1 hour more.
6. Preheat oven to 450°F (230°C) and bake buns for 15-20 minutes.

Yields: 2-3 dozen buns

Ranch Breads & Buns

Poppy Seed Swirls

This is a large recipe and the swirls keep in the freezer very well. Brush with an icing glaze before serving.

1 tbsp.	yeast (1 env. [7 g])	15 mL
½ cup	water	125 mL
1 tsp.	sugar	5 mL
1⅓ cups	butter	325 mL
⅓ cup	sugar	75 mL
1 tsp.	salt	5 mL
¾ cup	hot milk	175 mL
5-6 cups	all-purpose flour	1.25-1.5 L
2	eggs	2

Poppy Seed Filling:

1 cup	poppy seed, crushed	250 mL
¾ cup	milk	175 mL
3 tbsp.	chopped dates	45 mL
2 tbsp.	cream of wheat	30 mL
1 cup	brown sugar	250 mL

Icing Sugar Glaze:

½ cup	icing (confectioner's) sugar	125 mL
1 tbsp.	water	15 mL

1. Dissolve the yeast in water and sugar in the lukewarm water; let rise for 10 minutes.
2. Put butter, sugar and salt in the hot milk. Stir in some of the flour, then the eggs, then yeast mixture. Stir in enough of the remaining flour to make a soft dough; mix well.
3. Place dough in a large greased bowl; grease top of dough; cover and put in a warm place. Let rise until doubled in bulk, 1½-2 hours.
4. While dough is rising, prepare filling. Cook crushed poppy seed with milk, dates and brown sugar. Add cream of wheat and cook until thickened.
5. Preheat oven to 350°F (180°C).
6. Punch down dough and roll out into a 9 x 16" (23 x 41 cm) rectangle.

Poppy Seed Swirls continued

7. Spread filling lengthwise on one half of dough, fold other half over and pinch edge to seal. Cut into strips ½" (2.5 cm) wide. Hold ends of strips and twist (like a loose cork screw). Roll the twists into buns in a "snail" fashion. Place on cookie sheets and let rise 30 minutes, or until doubled in size. Bake for 10-12 minutes.
8. To make glaze, combine icing sugar and water.
9. Brush glaze over warm buns before serving.

Yields: 18-20 swirls

Walnut Filling: Crush 1 cup (250 mL) walnuts. Mix with 1 cup (250 mL) brown sugar and ⅓ cup (75 mL) butter and cinnamon.

Cranberry Orange Muffins

A wonderful way to use up leftover cranberry sauce, this unusual muffin has lots of health benefits as well!

3 cups	whole-wheat flour	750 mL
½ cup	honey	125 mL
2 tsp.	baking powder	10 mL
1 tsp.	salt	5 mL
1 tsp.	baking soda	5 mL
½ cup	fresh orange juice	125 mL
3 tsp.	vegetable oil OR melted shortening	15 mL
1	egg	1
2 cups	whole cranberry sauce (homemade OR canned)	500 mL
½ cup	water (optional, use only if cranberries seem quite dry)	125 mL

1. Preheat oven to 400°F (200°C).
2. Combine all ingredients in a large bowl. Add extra water of batter is too dry.
3. Fill greased or paper-lined muffin tins ⅔ full.
4. Bake for 15-20 minutes.

Yields: 2 dozen medium muffins

Rhubarb Oatmeal Muffins

These crunchy-topped little muffins go well with afternoon tea!

1 cup	all-purpose flour	250 mL
¾ cup	quick-cooking rolled oats	175 mL
½ cup	packed brown sugar	125 mL
2 tsp.	baking powder	10 mL
½ tsp.	baking soda	2 mL
¼ tsp.	salt	1 mL
¼ tsp.	nutmeg	1 mL
1 cup	finely diced rhubarb	250 mL
1 tsp.	grated orange rind	5 mL
⅓ cup	vegetable oil	75 mL
⅓ cup	orange juice	75 mL
1	egg	1

Crunchy Topping:

¼ cup	quick-cooking rolled oats	60 mL
¼ cup	packed brown sugar	60 mL
2 tbsp.	chopped nuts	30 mL
2 tbsp.	butter	30 mL
pinch	EACH of cinnamon and ginger	pinch

1. Preheat oven to 400°F (200°C).
2. In a large bowl, stir together flour, oats, brown sugar, baking powder, baking soda, salt and nutmeg.
3. Mix in rhubarb and orange rind.
4. Whisk together oil, juice and egg; add to flour mixture, stirring just until dry ingredients are moistened.
5. Spoon into paper-lined muffin tins.
6. To prepare topping, mix together all the ingredients and sprinkle over batter. Bake for 18 minutes, or until browned.

Yields: 12 medium muffins

Pictured on page 69.

Potato Biscuits

A wonderful way to use up leftover mashed potatoes. Serve with a stew.

1½ cups	all-purpose flour	375 mL
½ tsp.	salt	2 mL
1¼ cup	vegetable shortening	60 mL
1 cup	mashed potatoes	250 mL
1	egg, beaten	1

1. Preheat oven to 375°F (190°C).
2. Sift together flour and salt; cut in shortening until mixture resembles coarse crumbs.
3. Add mashed potatoes and egg. Knead dough lightly and roll or pat out to 1" (2.5 cm) thickness.
4. Cut dough into 6-8 rounds with a biscuit cutter or the open end of a water glass.
5. Bake on a greased cookie sheet for 15-20 minutes, or until slightly browned.

Yields: 6-8 biscuits

Variation: Cut any leftover biscuits in ¾" (2 cm) strips and serve as "soft" breadsticks.

Pictured on page 87.

Baking Powder Biscuits

Biscuits, a great western tradition, are always best eaten fresh and still slightly warm. Pour a white gravy over them for a southern breakfast dish

.2 cups	all-purpose flour	500 mL
2 tbsp.	baking powder	30 mL
½ tsp.	salt	2 mL
2 tbsp.	sugar	30 mL
½ tsp.	cream of tartar	2 mL
½ cup	shortening	125 mL
¾ cup	milk	175 mL
1	egg, beaten	1

1. Preheat oven to 425°F (220°C).
2. Sift dry ingredients into a bowl.
3. Blend in shortening until mixture resembles cornmeal or coarse crumbs.
4. Pour milk in slowly; add egg. Stir until mixture forms a stiff dough.
5. Turn dough out onto a floured board. Lightly knead for 5 minutes.
6. Roll dough out to ¾" (2 cm) thickness. Cut as desired into rounds or squares. Bake on an ungreased cookie sheet for 10-15 minutes.

Yields: 18-24 biscuits

Indian Bannock

These can easily be baked over a campfire. Best eaten warm right out of the pan, this is the ideal way to serve "bread" when on the trail or out camping, no need to transport any type of ordinary bread with you. Indians have used bannock in such a fashion for thousands of years. Delicious with butter and jam.

2 cups	all-purpose flour	500 mL
2 tsp.	baking powder	10 mL
1 tsp.	salt	5 mL
⅓ cup	oil	75 mL
⅔ cup	milk	150 mL

1. Preheat oven to 425°F (220°C).
2. Mix ingredients with a fork. Knead lightly.
3. Place in a greased 9" (23 cm) round pan or iron skillet.
    4. Bake until lightly browned, about 20 minutes.

Yields: 8-10 servings

Pictured on page 51.

Indian Bannock or Navajo Bread

This in an excellent bread to serve on the trail or while camping!

2 cups	all-purpose flour	500 mL
2 tsp.	baking powder	10 mL
3 tbsp.	powdered milk	45 mL
¼ tsp.	salt	1 mL
½ cup	chopped onion (optional)	125 mL
¾ cup	warm water	175 mL
	oil for frying	

1. Combine all dry ingredients; stir in warm water.
2. Mix and knead to make a moderately stiff dough. Cover and let rest 20-30 minutes.
3. Fill frying pan with oil 1½" (4 cm) deep; sprinkle a little salt in oil to keep it from burning; and heat on medium setting.
4. Pull off pieces of dough; roll them in a little flour; flatten with your hands and push a hole through the middle.
5. Fry dough in the hot oil, on both sides, until golden brown. Drain bannock on paper towel and eat immediately.

Yields: 6-8 bannock

Variation: Omit the onion, sprinkle sugar and cinnamon over the fried bread and use as a snack or dessert.

Trail Treat

This bread can be used to accompany any meal on the trail, camping, fishing or on a canoe trip, alone as a snack, or as a dessert. To roll out, use a bottle or can if there is no rolling pin available.

2 cups	all-purpose flour	500 mL
2 tsp.	baking powder	10 mL
dash	salt	dash
¾ cup	milk*	175 mL
	oil for frying	

Optional Toppings:

icing sugar
honey
cinnamon
syrup
jelly OR jam

1. Combine flour, baking powder, salt and enough milk to make a moderately stiff dough.
2. Knead until smooth, form into a ball. Cover and let rest for 30 minutes.
3. Flatten dough ball and cut across the circle 4 times to give you 8 equal wedges.
4. Roll each piece into an approximately 7" (18 cm) circle. Make a hole in the center of each piece.
5. Fry each circle in plenty of hot oil in a heavy skillet over medium heat until light brown, then turn the circle and brown remaining side.
6. Drain on paper towels. Serve hot.
7. Serve with any of the above mentioned topping options.

Make plenty!

Yields: 8 portions

* Dry skim milk powder and water may be substituted for milk.

Rise & Shine Bread

This breakfast bread is a favorite among our guests. No one has yet left the ranch without this recipe. It keeps moist and flavorful for a week in a cool place.

1 cup	all-purpose flour	250 mL
1 cup	whole-wheat flour	250 mL
¼ cup	sugar	60 mL
½ tsp.	salt	2 mL
1 tsp.	baking soda	5 mL
½ cup	raisins	125 mL
½ cup	coarsely chopped walnuts	125 mL
1 cup	crushed pineapple, undrained	250 mL
2 tbsp.	vegetable oil	30 mL
1	egg, beaten	1
1 tsp.	vanilla	5 mL

1. Preheat oven to 350°F (180°C).
2. In a large bowl, mix flours, sugar, salt, baking soda, raisins and walnuts; blend well.
3. In a separate bowl, combine pineapple, oil, egg and vanilla, blending well.
4. Combine dry and wet mixtures, stirring just enough to blend.
5. Pour batter into a greased and floured 5 x 9" (13 x 23 cm) bread pan and bake for 1 hour, or until done.

Yields: 1 loaf

Cottage Cheese Bread

This moist, slightly heavy bread, almost like a biscuit, is most delicious with a marmalade. It must be kept refrigerated.

4 cups	flour	1 L
4 tsp.	baking powder	20 mL
2 cups	cottage cheese, creamed in blender	500 mL
2 tsp.	sugar	10 mL
1 tsp.	salt	5 mL

1. Preheat oven to 350°F (180°C).
2. In a large bowl, sift flour and baking powder; add all other ingredients and mix well.
3. Press dough into a well-greased and floured 5 x 9" (13 x 23 cm) bread pan; let rest 15 minutes.
4. Bake for 1 hour and 15 minutes.

Yields: 1 loaf

Corny Rangers' Bread

Pass around hot squares of this golden bread with any evening meal, instead of dinner buns. It's also a wonderful breakfast treat with butter and honey or maple syrup.

2	eggs, beaten	2
2 cups	milk	500 mL
2 cups	cornmeal	500 mL
¾ cup	all-purpose flour	175 mL
4 tsp.	baking powder	20 mL
3 tbsp.	sugar	45 mL
½ tsp.	salt	2 mL

1. Preheat oven to 350°F (180°C). Butter a 9 x 13" (23 x 33 cm) baking pan.
2. Combine eggs and milk in a large bowl. Add cornmeal, flour, baking powder, sugar and salt and stir just until the dry ingredients are moistened.
3. Pour batter into the greased pan. Bake 30 minutes, or until top springs back when lightly pressed.

Yields: 9-10 servings

Trailside Corn Bread

Cook this corn bread in a cast-iron skillet over a campfire like the cowboys did.

4	slices bacon, diced	4
3 cups	yellow cornmeal	750 mL
1 tbsp.	all-purpose flour	15 mL
1½ tsp.	baking soda	7 mL
1½ tsp.	salt	7 mL
1 cup	buttermilk	250 mL
3	eggs, lightly beaten	3
14 oz.	can creamed corn	398 mL
1	small onion, diced	1

1. Preheat oven to 350°F (180°C).
2. Fry bacon until crispy, set aside.
3. In a medium bowl, combine the 4 dry ingredients, then add buttermilk, eggs and the creamed corn. Stir until smooth.
4. Add the bacon including the drippings; stir.
5. Pour into a well-greased 8" (20 cm) square baking pan and bake 30-35 minutes. OR pour into a well-greased cast-iron skillet and cook 30-35 minutes over a medium fire.

Yields: 9 servings

Variation: For a Mexican-style corn bread, add 1 small chopped jalapeño.

Pictured on page 121.

True love sprouts from the heart . . .
But it is nourished through the stomach . . .

Sweet Corn Bread

Corn bread was and still is a staple at ranches all over North America. Serve it with any type of stew or soup.It makes a refreshing change from other breads and it's so easy to make.

1 cup	flour	250 mL
1 tsp.	salt	5 mL
1 tbsp.	baking powder	15 ml
1 cup	cornmeal	250 mL
½ cup	brown sugar	125 mL
¾ cup	milk	175 mL
3 tbsp.	corn syrup	45 mL
1	egg, well beaten	1
2 tbsp.	vegetable oil	30 mL

1. Preheat oven to 425°F (220°C).
2. Combine flour, salt, baking powder, cornmeal and brown sugar in a mixing bowl.
3. Combine milk, syrup and egg and pour into blended dry ingredients.
4. Add oil. Stir just to blend.
5. Pour batter into greased 8" (20 cm) square pan. Bake for 20 minutes.

Yields: 9 servings

Midday Roundup

(Lunches)

41

Summer Luncheon Salad

This unusual chunky chicken (or turkey) salad is ideal for picnics and potlucks, or to make ahead if you are going to have a busy day. It can be made up to 1 day ahead.

2 cups	cooked, cubed chicken OR turkey	500 mL
½ cup	cubed Swiss cheese	125 mL
1 cup	sliced celery	250 mL
¾ cup	cored, cubed unpeeled tart red apples	175 mL
⅓ cup	honey-roasted almonds, slightly crushed	75 mL

Honey Yogurt Sauce:

½ cup	plain yogurt	125 mL
¼ cup	sour cream	60 mL
2 tbsp.	honey	30 mL
1 tbsp.	minced parsley	15 mL
1 tsp.	ground mustard seeds	5 mL
1 tsp.	lemon juice	5 mL

1. Toss all salad ingredients, except almonds, in a large bowl.
2. Cover and refrigerate.
3. Combine all sauce ingredients. Refrigerate.
4. At serving time combine salad and the Honey Yogurt Sauce.
5. Sprinkle with honey-roasted almonds.

Yields: 4-6 servings

Serve with one of the corn bread recipes on pages 38, 39 and 40.

Vegetable – Turkey Salad

This gourmet salad can be served as a main dish with bannock or cornbread. The dressing is delicious.

8	slices bacon	8
⅓ cup	plain yogurt	75 mL
2 tbsp.	mayonnaise OR salad dressing	30 mL
1 tsp.	chopped fresh dill OR ¼ tsp. (1 mL) dried dillweed	5 mL
¼ tsp.	salt	1 mL
dash	pepper	dash
2	green onions, sliced	2
3 cups	cooked, cubed turkey OR chicken	750 mL
2 cups	tiny cauliflower florets	500 mL
¼ cup	sliced radishes	60 mL
1	medium avocado, cut into 12 slices (optional)	1

1. Cook bacon until crisp, then drain and crumble.
2. Mix yogurt, mayonnaise, dillweed, salt, pepper and onions in a large bowl.
3. Add turkey, bacon, cauliflower and radishes.
4. Toss, cover and refrigerate 1-2 hours, or until chilled.
5. Serve on individual plates and garnish with avocado slices, if desired.

Yields: 4-6 servings

We may live without poetry, music or art . . .

We may live without conscience,

We may live without heart . . .

We may live without friends,

We may live without books . . .

But civilized people cannot live without cooks!!!

Terrific Tuna Salad

This is a real pleaser with crunchy vegetables adding color and texture.

2 cups	uncooked pasta*	500 mL
2 x 6 oz.	cans water-packed tuna, drained and flaked	2 x 170 g
¼ cup	sliced celery	60 mL
¼ cup	carrots in thin strips	60 mL
¼ cup	chopped, seeded cucumber	60 mL
¼ cup	thinly sliced radishes	60 mL
2 tbsp.	chopped green onions	30 mL
1 tbsp.	sweet pickle relish	15 mL

Yogurt Dressing:

½ cup	plain yogurt	125 mL
½ cup	mayonnaise	125 mL
1 tsp.	lemon pepper	5 mL

1. Cook pasta to desired tenderness. Drain, rinse with cold water.
2. In a large bowl, combine all salad ingredients; toss gently.
3. In a small bowl, combine the dressing ingredients.
4. Pour dressing over salad, and toss gently to coat. Cover and refrigerate 1-2 hours to blend flavors. Store in refrigerator.

Yields: 4 servings

* Try various pasta shapes, fusilli twists, shells or bows to make a decorative addition to this salad.

Shrimp Surprise

Here is a simple and very showy luncheon dish. Team it with the Cottage Cheese Bread on page 38.

⅓ cup	mayonnaise	75 mL
1 tsp.	prepared mustard	5 mL
1 tsp.	chopped dillweed	5 mL
¼ tsp.	sugar	1 mL
½ tsp.	salt	2 mL
¼ tsp.	coarse pepper	1 mL
12	large shrimp, cooked, halved	12
6	eggs, hard-cooked, peeled, cut in 1" (2.5 cm) pieces	6
⅓ cup	chopped green onions, in 1" (2.5 cm) pieces	75 mL
2	celery stalks, chopped	2
½ cup	cooked peas	125 mL
	lettuce leaves	

1. In a large bowl, mix mayonnaise, mustard, dill, sugar, salt and pepper; blend well.
2. Add shrimp, eggs, onions, celery and peas. Stir gently until well coated. Cover and refrigerate 2 hours.
3. Serve on lettuce leaves.

Yields: 4-6 servings

German-Style Fusilli Salad

5	slices bacon, finely chopped	5
1	small onion, finely chopped	1
1	small red pepper, diced	1
1	small green pepper, diced	1
1 cup	chicken broth	250 mL
¼ cup	vinegar	60 mL
2 tbsp.	lemon juice	30 mL
1 tbsp.	vegetable oil	15 mL
1 tbsp.	Dijon mustard	15 mL
13 oz.	pkg. fusilli pasta	375 g
4	hard-boiled eggs, chopped	4
¼ cup	chopped fresh parsley	60 mL

1. In a medium skillet, cook bacon until crisp. Remove bacon; drain on paper towels and set aside. Drain all but 1 tbsp. (15 mL) bacon fat from skillet; sauté onion until tender.
2. Stir in red and green peppers, broth, vinegar, lemon juice, oil and mustard; heat through.
3. Cook fusilli according to package directions; drain.
4. Toss fusilli with vegetable mixture. Add reserved bacon, hard-cooked eggs and parsley; toss gently. Serve warm or at room temperature.

Yields: 6 servings

Pictured on page 121.

Pita Lunch

The blessings of pita bread! Those handy little bread-pockets are perfect for lunches and snacks, summer or winter. So versatile and so easy!

Here and in the following recipes are a few fillings we use very successfully at the ranch.

1 lb.	ground beef	500 g
1	onion, chopped	1
1	garlic clove, crushed	1
½ tsp.	caraway seed	2 mL
½ tsp.	salt	2 mL
¼ tsp.	pepper	1 mL
2 cups	shredded lettuce	500 mL
2	small tomatoes, chopped	2
1 cup	finely chopped cucumbers	250 mL
4	pita breads, 6" (15 cm) diameter	4

1. In a large skillet, brown meat, onion, garlic and caraway seed until all pink color has disappeared from meat; drain. Stir in salt and pepper.
2. Combine lettuce, tomatoes and cucumbers.
3. Cut each pita bread in half crossways; open halves to form pockets.
4. Spoon hamburger mixture into pita pockets. Top with lettuce, tomato and cucumber mixture.
5. Spoon Yogurt Mayonnaise Sauce, page 80, over pita filling.

Yields: 4 servings

Midday Roundup

Chicken Pita

Another variation for pita breads. Try some of your own combinations.

4	pita breads, 6" (15 cm) diameter	4
1½cups	chopped cooked chicken OR turkey	375 mL
½ cup	finely chopped celery	125 mL
½ cup	finely chopped lettuce	125 mL
¼ cup	chopped green onions	60 mL
¼ cup	chopped red pepper	60 mL
	salt and pepper to taste	

1. Cut each pita bread in half crossways; open halves to form pockets.
2. Mix all remaining ingredients; spoon into pita pockets.
3. Spoon Yogurt Mayonnaise Sauce, page 80, over pita filling.

Yields: 4 servings

Seafood Pita

A creative way to use any type of leftover fish or seafood. Make sure to remove all bones.

4	pita breads, 6" (15 cm) diameter	4
1½ cups	cooked seafood, in pieces no smaller than 1" (2.5 cm)	375 mL
½ cup	finely chopped celery	125 mL
¼ cup	finely chopped green onions	60 mL
½ cup	finely chopped lettuce	125 mL
1 tsp.	chopped dillweed	5 mL
	salt and pepper to taste	
2 tsp.	tangy seafood sauce, page 135, OR commercial seafood sauce	10 mL

1. Cut each pita bread in half crossways; open halves to form pockets.
2. Combine all remaining ingredients, except seafood sauce.
3. Spoon filling into pita pockets.
4. Add seafood sauce to Yogurt Mayonnaise Sauce, page 80, and drizzle over pita filling.

Yields: 4 servings

Salmon on a Bun

A wonderful way to introduce Canadian salmon – on a small scale – to the European tourist. Easy, fast and perfect on hot days.

7.5 oz.	can salmon, drained	13 g
½ cup	mayonnaise OR salad dressing	125 mL
½ cup	chopped celery	125 mL
¼ cup	sliced green onion	60 mL
¼ tsp.	salt	1 mL
¼ tsp.	pepper	1 mL
4	French rolls OR frankfurter buns, split	4
	tomato slices	
	chopped parsley	
	radishes	

1. Combine all ingredients, except rolls, tomato, parsley and radishes.
2. Fill rolls with salmon mixture.
3. Place a fresh tomato slice on top of each roll; sprinkle with parsley – looks and tastes great!

Yields: 4 servings

Serve with fresh radishes or sweet pickles.

Grilled European Wieners with Onion-Sauerkraut Relish

Without a doubt, this is a favorite with our German guests. In no time they feel at home.

Onion-Sauerkraut Relish:

¼ cup	oil	60 mL
½ cup	sugar	125 mL
2 cups	chopped onions	500 mL
2 cups	chopped sauerkraut	500 mL
½ cup	cider vinegar	125 mL
¼ tsp.	salt	1 mL
½ tsp.	caraway seed	2 mL
8	European wieners	8
2 cups	beer	500 mL
8	Italian buns	8

1. To make the relish, heat oil in a large skillet over medium heat; add sugar, onions and well-drained sauerkraut. Cook 15 minutes, until slightly browned.
2. Add vinegar, salt and caraway seed. Put the lid on the skillet and simmer for another 15 minutes.
3. Serve relish immediately (warm), or cover and refrigerate for up to 3 weeks.
4. To prepare wieners, preheat grill*. In a large saucepan, combine beer and wieners.
5. Heat, but do not boil. Cover and simmer for 10 minutes.
6. Place wieners on the grill and barbecue over medium heat for 6-10 minutes.
7. Serve wieners on Italian buns and top with Onion-Sauerkraut Relish.

Yields: 8 servings

* Wieners may also be grilled over a campfire . . . pass the beer!!!!

Midday Roundup (Lunch)

Corn Chowder with Fresh Herbs & Smoked Ham, page 62

Crispy Corn & Radish Salad, page 75

Indian Bannock, page 34

Cowboy Coffee, page 8

Cordon Bleu Casserole

This delectable combination of turkey, ham and cheese with a crunchy topping is ideal for lunch or a light supper.

4 cups	cubed cooked turkey	1 L
3 cups	cubed fully cooked ham	750 mL
1 cup	shredded Cheddar cheese	250 mL
1 cup	chopped onion	250 mL
¼ cup	butter OR margarine	60 mL
⅓ cup	all-purpose flour	75 mL
2 cups	light cream	500 mL
1 tsp.	dry dillweed	5 mL
⅛ tsp.	dry mustard	0.5 mL
⅛ tsp.	ground nutmeg	0.5 mL

Cheddar Dill Topping:

1 cup	dry bread crumbs	250 mL
2 tbsp.	melted butter OR margarine	30 mL
¼ tsp.	dry dillweed	1 mL
¼ cup	shredded Cheddar cheese	60 mL
¼ cup	chopped walnuts	60 mL

1. In a large bowl, combine turkey, ham and cheese; set aside.
2. In a saucepan, sauté onion in butter until tender. Add flour; stir to form a paste.
3. Gradually add cream, stirring constantly. Bring to a boil and boil 1 minute, or until thick.
4. Add dillweed, mustard and nutmeg, mix well.
5. Remove the sauce from the heat and pour over meat mixture.
6. Spoon meat mixture into a greased 9 x 13" (23 x 33 cm) baking dish. Toss bread crumbs, butter and dillweed; stir in cheese and walnuts. Sprinkle over the casserole.
7. Bake, uncovered, at 350°F (180°C) for 30 minutes, or until heated through.

Yields: 8-10 servings

*Campfires and covered wagons
   at Barrier Chaparral Ranch*

Roper's Blintzes

A crêpe-like wrapper encases a cream cheese filling. Blintzes taste heavenly with grilled fish or chicken and a cucumber salad. They are a super dish for potluck suppers!! This recipe can be doubled.

Blintz Batter:

2	eggs, well beaten	2
1½ cups	milk	375 mL
1 tbsp.	sugar	15 mL
¼ tsp.	vanilla	1 mL
1¼ cups	flour	300 mL
1½ tsp.	baking powder	7 mL
¼ tsp.	salt	1 mL

Dilled Cheese Filling:

2 cups	creamed cottage cheese	500 mL
2	eggs, well beaten	2
¼ tsp.	salt	1 mL
1 tbsp.	sugar	15 mL
1 tbsp.	chopped dillweed, fresh OR dried	15 mL
	cereal OR whipping cream	

1. To make batter, mix eggs, milk and sugar. Add vanilla.
2. Sift flour, baking powder and salt together and add to milk mixture, stirring until smooth. I use an electric beater for this.
3. Heat a greased 8-10" (20-25 cm) frying pan. Pour in a small amount of batter (depending on pan size). Tilt pan to spread batter to make very thin pancakes. Cook until top is dry and bottom is slightly browned; turn cakes and cook on the other side for about 15 seconds. Repeat until all batter is used.
4. To make filling, mix cottage cheese, eggs, salt, sugar and dillweed.
5. Spread each pancake with filling and roll up like a jelly roll. Cut into desired lengths and arrange in a well-buttered 9 x 13" (23 x 33 cm) deep-dish casserole; pour on enough sweet cream to almost cover the blintzes, leave at least 2" (5 cm) space; cream will bubble and blintzes will puff up.
6. Bake at 275°F (140°C) for 35 minutes. Uncover towards the end so that blintzes brown a little.

Yields: 18-20 blintzes

See Alternate Methods & Serving Suggestions on the next page.

Roper's Blintzes *continued*

Alternate Methods & Serving Suggestions:

1. The blintzes can be made and filled ahead of time and kept frozen up to 2 months. When ready to serve, place filled blintzes in casserole, cover with sweet cream and bake. Extend baking time 15 minutes if blintzes are frozen.
2. Roper's Blintzes can easily be made into a sweet dish and they taste wonderful as a breakfast dish. Omit the dill and double the sugar. Sprinkle with cinnamon just before baking. Serve hot.

Spicy Broiled Shrimp

¼ cup	butter OR margarine	60 mL
2 tbsp.	vegetable oil	30 mL
1 tsp.	hot pepper sauce	5 mL
1 tsp.	dried rosemary, crushed	5 mL
2	garlic cloves, minced	2
¼ tsp.	crushed dried parsley	1 mL
¼ tsp.	crushed dried basil	1 mL
¼ tsp.	crushed dried oregano	1 mL
1½ lbs.	large, fresh shrimp, peeled and deveined	750 g

1. In a small saucepan, melt butter over low heat.
2. Add all remaining ingredients except shrimp; cook, uncovered, for 5 minutes.
3. Rinse shrimp; pat dry with paper towels. Place on broiler pan. brush generously with melted butter mixture.
4. Broil, 5" (13 cm) from heat source, until shrimp turns pink, turning and brushing frequently with melted butter mixture. Do not over cook or shrimp will be tough.
5. Garnish as desired.
6. Spoon remaining melted butter mixture over cooked shrimp.

Yields: 6 servings

Serve with lemon wedges and one of the corn breads on pages 38, 39 and 40.

Skillet Paella

A platter with cut-up vegetables is wonderful with this. I have served this shortcut version of the famous Spanish specialty for many years for lunch and it has always enjoyed great popularity.

12 oz.	pkg. large frozen peeled shrimp	340 g
10 oz.	pkg. frozen green peas	283 g
19 oz.	can whole tomatoes, undrained	540 mL
2 cups	cooked instant rice	500 mL
¼ cup	finely chopped onion	60 mL
1 tsp.	chicken bouillon granules	5 mL
1 tsp.	paprika	5 mL
¼ tsp.	cayenne	1 mL

1. Rinse frozen shrimp and peas with cold water to separate; drain. Remove hard tail ends from shrimp and cut the shrimp in half.
2. Combine all ingredients in a 12" (30 cm) skillet; break up tomatoes.
3. Heat paella to boiling, stirring occasionally; reduce heat.
4. Simmer, uncovered, 5 minutes; remove from heat.
5. Cover tightly and let stand 10 minutes.

Yields: 6-8 servings

Soup "will do" on cool days

Howdy Bean Soup

This recipe comes from early settlers who brought it to this country. Very often it was one of the few dishes they could afford. I have modernized it somewhat and it has become a favorite among our guests.

2 cups	dry navy beans, soaked over night	500 mL
3	bay leaves	3
2 cups	beef stock	500 mL
2 cups	shredded cabbage	500 mL
2	leeks, cut in 2" (5 cm) lengths OR 1 large onion, sliced	2
2	medium potatoes, cubed	2
2	medium carrots, thickly sliced	2
¼ tsp.	nutmeg	1 mL
	salt and pepper to taste	
5	Bavarian smokies, thickly sliced	5
2 tbsp.	chopped cilantro OR parsley	30 mL

1. Place beans in a large Dutch oven; add beef stock and add water to cover beans generously. Add bay leaves and bring to a boil. Simmer for 1 hour.
2. Add cabbage, leeks, potatoes, carrots, nutmeg and salt and pepper to taste. Add water to cover vegetables. Bring to a boil and simmer 30 minutes, or until vegetables are tender.
3. Add sliced smokies and simmer another 10 minutes.
4. Remove soup from heat and sprinkle with cilantro or parsley.

Yields: 6-8 servings

Serve hot with the Cottage Cheese Bread on page 38.

Soup "will do" on cool days

Jean's White Bean & Sauerkraut Soup

Many years ago when we visited my sister-in-law, Jean, in Winnipeg, she made us this delicious combination of beans and sauerkraut. This is a very old and popular Ukrainian dish. Serve it for lunch or for supper. It is very comforting on cold winter days, and very rich in fiber.

1 cup	dry white beans	250 mL
½ lb.	spareribs	250 g
8 cups	water	2 L
1	medium potato, chopped	1
1	carrot, sliced	1
½ cup	chopped mushrooms, fresh OR canned	125 mL
3 cups	sauerkraut	750 mL
1	medium onion, chopped	1
1 tbsp.	vegetable oil	15 mL
½ cup	cream (optional)	125 mL
	salt and pepper to taste	
	chopped dillweed	

1. Wash white beans and soak overnight; drain. Wash the meat; cover with water; add beans, and simmer until meat is tender, about 60 minutes. With long cooking some more water may be needed.
2. Add potato and carrot and continue simmering until vegetables are tender. Add mushrooms and sauerkraut. If the sauerkraut is very sour, rinse it in cold water before adding to soup.
3. Simmer the soup until the sauerkraut is tender. If using canned mushrooms, add the mushroom liquid to the soup, also.
4. Sauté the onion in hot oil until translucent; add to soup.
5. Add the cream if using, season to taste with salt, pepper and dillweed.
6. Serve the meat as separate course or place a small slice of meat in each bowl of soup.

Yields: 6 servings

This soup is usually served with rye bread.

Soup "will do" on cool days

Grandma's Potato Soup
(with Ukrainian Sausage or European Wieners)

This is a delicious, hearty soup. Suitable as a main dish or lunch, it is excellent reheated.

4-6	medium potatoes, peeled and quartered	4-6
3	bay leaves	3
8	whole peppercorns	8
1 tsp.	salt	5 mL
3-4	carrots, thickly sliced	3-4
2	celery stalks, thickly sliced (include leaves if available)	2
1	small onion, coarsely chopped	1
2	parsnips, peeled and thickly sliced	2
1 tsp.	salt	5 mL
¼ tsp.	pepper	1 mL
2 tsp.	lemon juice	10 mL
6	slices bacon, finely chopped	6
1	onion, finely chopped	1
1 lb.	Ukrainian sausage, thickly sliced OR whole European wieners, 1 per serving	500 g
2 tsp.	chopped fresh parsley	10 mL
1 tsp.	chopped fresh dillweed	10 mL
	salt and pepper to taste	

1. In a medium-sized pot, combine first 4 ingredients, cover with water and boil until tender. Remove bay leaves and peppercorns; mash coarsely and set aside.
2. In a large pot, combine next 7 ingredients, cover with water and boil for 15 minutes.
3. Fry bacon until crisp; remove from pan. Sauté chopped onion in bacon fat until translucent; remove onion from pan; discard bacon fat. Combine mashed potato, vegetables, including vegetable broth, fried bacon, onion and sausage. Mix well and bring to a boil, stirring occasionally. If the soup seems too thick, add more water. Turn off heat, add parsley and dillweed, let flavors blend for 10 minutes. Season to taste with salt and pepper.

Yields: 6-8 servings

Soup "will do" on cool days

Settler's Green Bean Soup

Early settlers brought this soup from the old country over 100 years ago.

½ lb.	oxtail	250 g
4	whole peppercorns	4
2	bay leaves	2
1 tsp.	salt	5 mL
1½ lbs.	fresh OR frozen green beans, in 1" (2.5 cm) pieces	750 g
2 lbs.	potatoes, cubed	1 kg
1	large onion, halved and sliced	1
1 tbsp.	savory, dry OR fresh	15 mL
1 tbsp.	chopped green onions	15 mL
2 tbsp.	chopped fresh parsley	30 mL
	salt and pepper to taste	

1. Cover oxtail in plenty of water, add peppercorns, bay leaves and 1 tsp. (5 mL) salt. Cook until oxtail is tender, about 45 minutes.
2. Remove meat and strain stock. Return stock to pot.
3. Add beans, potatoes, onion and savory to stock; cook 30 minutes.
4. Remove meat from bones and add meat to soup.
5. When ready to serve add green onions, parsley and salt and pepper to taste.

Yields: 6-8 servings

Golden Carrot Soup

There are always requests for seconds. Serve with baking powder biscuits.

¼ cup	butter	60 mL
1	medium onion, sliced	1
1	garlic clove, minced	1
5 cups	chicken stock	1.25 L
2½ cups	sliced carrots	625 mL
¼ cup	long-grain rice	60 mL
	salt and chopped parsley	
½ cup	cream OR milk, or more to thin	125 mL

1. Melt butter in a saucepan. Sauté onion and garlic until tender. Add stock, carrots and rice. Bring to a boil. Cover and simmer 45 minutes.
3. In small batches, blend (purée) vegetables until smooth.
4. Reheat purée in saucepan; thin with water if necessary; add salt and parsley to taste. Add cream when serving.

Yields: 4 servings

Soup "will do" on cool days

Corn Chowder with Fresh Herbs & Smoked Ham

4 cups	chicken broth	1 L
½ cup	finely chopped onion	125 mL
3 cups	diced potatoes	750 mL
4 cups	whole kernel corn	1 L
1	medium carrot, finely chopped	1
1	bay leaf	1
1	sprig EACH fresh thyme and tarragon	1
¼ cup	milk	60 mL
¼ cup	cereal OR whipping cream	60 mL
2 tbsp.	canned pimientos, drained and diced	30 mL
3 tbsp.	chopped fresh parsley	45 mL
1 cup	julienne-cut smoked ham	250 mL
	pepper (optional)	
	additional chopped fresh parsley	

1. In a large saucepan, combine broth, onion, 1½ cups (375 mL) of the potatoes, 2 cups (500 mL) of the corn and the carrot.
2. Tie together bay leaf, thyme and tarragon to make a bouquet garni. Add to saucepan and bring to a boil; reduce heat and simmer 20 minutes.
3. Remove bay leaf and bouquet garni. Purée soup in small batches in electric blender until smooth. Return soup to saucepan, stir in the rest of the potatoes and remaining corn and bring to a boil.
4. Reduce heat and simmer 15 minutes. Add milk, cream, pimientos, parsley and ham. Heat through.
5. Season with pepper, if desired. Ladle soup into bowls; garnish with additional chopped parsley.

Yields   6-8 servings

   Serve with biscuits or corn bread.

Pictured on page 51.

Soup "will do" on cool days

Cauliflower or Broccoli Cream Soup

This flavorful soup is a gourmet dish in Europe. When you are travelling, if you see it on the menu, be sure to order it. I have served it to our guests for many years and there are always requests for seconds.

1	small head of cauliflower OR	1
	3 stalks of broccoli	
3 tbsp.	butter	45 mL
2 tbsp.	flour	30 mL
1½ cups	milk	375 mL
½ cup	cream	125 mL
1 tbsp.	chopped cilantro OR parsley	15 mL
	salt and pepper to taste	
1	large onion, thinly sliced	1
½ cup	croûtons	125 mL
	Parmesan cheese	

1. Clean cauliflower or broccoli, cut into large chunks. In a medium saucepan, cover with water and cook 15-20 minutes, or until vegetables are tender.
2. Mash vegetables or purée in an electric blender.
3. In a large Dutch oven, heat 2 tbsp. (30 mL) butter. Stir in the flour. Slowly add the milk, stirring continuously.
4. Add the vegetable purée and bring to a boil. Remove from heat, add cream, parsley, salt and pepper to taste.
5. Melt 1 tbsp. (15 mL) butter in a small frying pan and slightly brown onion slices. Add to soup. If the soup is too thick add more milk or water.
6. When ready to serve, top individual bowls of soup with croûtons and sprinkle with Parmesan cheese.

Yields: 4-6 servings

Kasandra: "What are you doing,
standing so still?"

Gloria: "I'm trying a new recipe.
It says do not stir for 10 minutes."

Soup "will do" on cool days

63

Gazpacho

Try this hearty cold soup on a hot day!!! It's refreshing, colorful and flavorful.

2 cups	puréed tomatoes	500 mL
1¾ cups	tomato juice	425 mL
⅔ cup	peeled, seeded, finely chopped cucumber	150 mL
½ cup	finely chopped green pepper	125 mL
½ cup	finely chopped onion	125 mL
2 tbsp.	red wine vinegar	30 mL
1 tbsp.	Italian dressing	15 mL
1 tbsp.	lemon juice	15 mL
1	garlic clove, minced	1
½ tsp.	pepper	2 mL
2 tsp.	sugar	10 mL
1 tsp.	salt	5 mL
	few drops hot sauce (optional)	
	chopped green onions for garnish	
	cucumber slices for garnish	
	oil and garlic croûtons for garnish	

1. Combine all the ingredients, except the garnishes, in a large bowl; stir well. Cover and chill at least 8 hours. To serve, ladle soup into individual bowls and garnish with chopped green onion, thinly sliced cucumbers and croûtons.

Yields: 4-6 servings

Soup "will do" on cool days

Munchies & Crunchies

(Salads)

Special Potato Salad

Vinegar and yogurt add a refreshing tang to the crispness of the onion and celery and the heartiness of the eggs and crumbled bacon. A true delight – our guests love it!

2½ lbs.	red potatoes	1 kg
2 tbsp.	red wine vinegar	30 mL
1 tbsp.	olive OR vegetable oil	15 mL
1 tbsp.	prepared mustard	15 mL
½ tsp.	dried basil	2 mL
½ tsp.	pepper	2 mL
1 tsp.	salt	5 mL
½ cup	plain yogurt	125 mL
¼ cup	sour cream	60 mL
1	garlic clove, crushed	1
1 cup	chopped red onion	250 mL
¾ cup	diced celery	175 mL
4	bacon strips, cooked and crumbled	4
3	hard-cooked eggs, chopped	3

1. In a large saucepan, cook potatoes in boiling salted water until tender.
2. While potatoes are cooking, in a large bowl, combine vinegar, oil, mustard, basil, pepper and salt; mix well.
3. Drain potatoes; cut into 1" (2.5 cm) chunks and add to vinegar and oil mixture while still warm.
4. In another bowl, combine yogurt, sour cream and garlic. Add onion, celery, bacon and eggs; mix well.
5. Add yogurt mixture to potato mixture; toss gently. Cover and chill for several hours.

Yields: 6-8 servings

Bacon & Egg Potato Salad

You can't beat the tasty combination of flavors in this salad!! Best of all you can make it a day ahead.

5 cups	cooked, peeled, cubed potatoes	1.25 L
¼ cup	chopped green onions	60 mL
½ cup	finely chopped celery	125 mL
⅓ cup	lemon juice	75 mL
⅓ cup	water	75 mL
¼ cup	vegetable oil	60 mL
1 tsp.	Worcestershire sauce	5 mL
½ tsp.	dry mustard	2 mL
½ tsp.	salt	2 mL
¼ tsp.	pepper	1 mL
4-5	slices bacon, cooked, crumbled	4-5
3	hard-boiled eggs, chopped	3
¼ cup	grated Parmesan cheese	60 mL
3 tbsp.	chopped parsley	45 mL

1. In a large bowl, combine potatoes, onions and celery.
2. In a small saucepan, combine lemon juice, water, oil, salt, Worcestershire sauce, mustard and pepper; bring to a boil.
3. Pour over potato mixture, mix well.
4. Cover salad and chill overnight to blend flavors.
5. Remove salad from refrigerator 30 minutes before serving; stir in bacon, eggs, Parmesan cheese and parsley.

Yields: 10-12 servings

Happiness is like a potato salad . . .

Share it and you have a picnic . . .

Calico Corn Salad

This colorful salad will keep well in the refrigerator for 5-6 days.

4 cups	fresh corn kernels, 6-7 medium cobs	1 L
½ cup	vegetable oil	125 mL
¼ cup	cider vinegar	60 mL
2 tbsp..	lemon juice	30 mL
¼ cup	minced fresh parsley	60 mL
1 tbsp.	sugar	15 mL
1 tsp.	salt	5 mL
	sprinkle of cayenne pepper	
2	large tomatoes, seeded and chopped	2
½ cup	chopped onion	125 mL
½ cup	chopped green pepper	125 mL
½ cup	chopped sweet red pepper	125 mL

1. In a large saucepan, cook corn in enough water to cover for 5-7 minutes, or until tender.
2. Drain corn; cool and set aside.
3. In a large bowl, mix the oil, vinegar, lemon juice, parsley, sugar, salt and a sprinkle of cayenne pepper.
4. Cut cooled corn off the cobs.
5. Add corn, tomatoes, onion and peppers to the oil mixture. Mix well. Cover and chill for several hours or overnight.

Yields: 10 servings

Sweet Snacking
Rhubarb Oatmeal Muffins, page 32
Peach Kuchen, page 182
Ranch-Style Gingerbread Cookies, page 164
Pumpkin Dip, page 164

Cauliflower Salad with Capers

This is a very old recipe that my mother used to make. Capers are pickled flower buds from a bush found around the Mediterranean. Available in most supermarkets, they have a zesty, pungent flavor. This salad tastes very refreshing and gives an exotic touch to ordinary cauliflower.

1	medium cauliflower	1

Lemon Caper Dressing:

½ cup	lemon juice	125 mL
¼ cup	vegetable oil	60 mL
½ tsp.	salt	2 mL
2 tbsp.	caper juice	30 mL
1 tbsp.	capers	15 mL
1 tbsp.	chopped fresh dillweed	15 mL

1. Break cauliflower into florets. In a large saucepan bring water to a boil; add cauliflower and boil for 5 minutes. Drain. Carefully transfer cauliflower to a serving bowl.
2. With a wire whisk, blend lemon juice, oil, salt and the caper juice; add capers and dill, blend. Spoon Lemon Caper Dressing over warm cauliflower and marinate for 2 hours at room temperature.
3. Spoon marinade over cauliflower 2-3 times.

Yields: *6 servings*

This salad is wonderful with Greek ribs, barbecued fish, chicken or pork.

Pictured on page 157.

"Horsing Around" at
Barrier Chaparral Ranch.

Green Pea Salad

If you are looking for a side dish that adds color to any meal, this is it!!

3 cups	fresh OR frozen peas	750 mL
6	slices bacon	6
½ cup	mayonnaise OR salad dressing	125 mL
⅛ tsp.	pepper	0.5 mL
½ tsp.	dillweed	2 mL
1 tsp.	sugar	5 mL
1 tsp.	prepared mustard	5 mL

1. If using fresh peas, steam and cool. Pour hot water over frozen peas, just to thaw. Drain.
2. Fry bacon until crispy. Drain bacon and crumble. Set aside.
3. Combine mayonnaise, pepper, dillweed, sugar and prepared mustard.
4. Stir peas and bacon together. Pour dressing over peas and stir to coat.

Yields: 6 servings

Broccoli Bacon Salad

1	large broccoli, cut into florets (about 4 cups [1 L])	1
1	small red onion, coarsely chopped	1
1 cup	raisins (optional)	250 mL
10-12	slices bacon, cooked and crumbled	10-12

Dressing:

3 tbsp.	vinegar	45 mL
⅓ cup	mayonnaise	75 mL
⅓ cup	sugar	75 mL

1. In a large serving bowl, combine the broccoli, onion, raisins and bacon; set aside.
2. In a mixing bowl, combine dressing ingredients.
    3. Just before serving, pour dressing over broccoli mixture; toss to coat.

Yields: 4 servings

Variation: Try half broccoli and half cauliflower florets for a tasty, colorful variation. Slivers of red pepper also add flavor and eye appeal.

Dilled Cucumber Salad

A delightfully different salad, crisp cucumber and mellow rich avocado spiced with cider vinegar.

1	medium English cucumber, unpeeled, sliced	1
1	medium red onion, thinly sliced	1
2	avocados, peeled and sliced	2

Garlic Dill Dressing:

¼ cup	cider vinegar	60 mL
½ cup	salad oil	125 mL
1	garlic clove, crushed	1
1 tsp.	chopped dillweed	5 mL
	salt and pepper to taste	
	lettuce leaves (optional)	

1. Place cucumber, onion and avocados in a shallow dish.
2. Combine vinegar, oil and seasonings. Whip with a wire whisk until mixed. Pour over vegetables and chill 2 hours. Turn occasionally. Serve on lettuce leaves if desired.

Yields: 4-6 servings

Yogurt Cucumber Salad

We have prepared cucumbers in many different ways, but this one is the winner.

Creamy Dressing:

¼ cup	mayonnaise	60 mL
¼ cup	plain yogurt	60 mL
2 tsp.	sugar	10 mL
½ tsp.	salt	2 mL
1	long English cucumber, unpeeled, sliced	1
1 tsp.	chopped dillweed	5 mL
1 tbsp.	chopped green onion	15 mL

1. With a wire whisk, blend all sauce ingredients well.
2. Add sliced cucumbers.
3. Sprinkle dillweed and onions over cucumbers for garnish.

Yields: 4 servings

Cucumber Slaw

This salad can be made the day before serving and refrigerated overnight, if you wish.

3	long English cucumbers	3
6	large carrots	6
⅓ cup	vegetable oil	75 mL
⅓ cup	white vinegar	75 mL
⅓ cup	granulated sugar	75 mL
¾ tsp.	salt	3 mL
¼ tsp.	pepper	1 mL
⅓ cup	chopped fresh dill OR 1 tbsp. (15 mL) dried	75 mL

1. Slice unpeeled cucumbers lengthwise in half and scoop out seeds with a spoon. Cut cucumber into matchstick pieces, 1½" (4 cm) in length and ¼" (1 cm) thick.
2. Peel carrots and slice into similar matchsticks.
3. Place vegetables in a large bowl. Whisk oil, vinegar, sugar, salt and pepper together. Stir in dill. Pour dressing over vegetables and stir until mixed.
4. Cover salad and refrigerate until ready to take to the picnic.

Yields: 8-10 servings

Creamy Coleslaw

This colorful and tasty coleslaw is a favorite at the ranch. When this is put on the table it disappears quickly.

Coleslaw Dressing:

½ cup	mayonnaise OR salad dressing	125 mL
¼ cup	milk OR vegetable oil	60 mL
¼ cup	vinegar	60 mL
3 tbsp.	sugar	45 mL
	salt and pepper to taste	

Coleslaw:

4 cups	shredded cabbage	1 L
1	carrot, grated	1
½ cup	diced onion OR green onion	125 mL
1	small red apple, diced, with peel	1

Creamy Coleslaw continued

1. Place dressing ingredients in a jar or plastic container and shake well. Dressing will keep in refrigerator. Shake before using.
2. Combine cabbage, carrot, onions and apple in a large bowl.
3. Pour dressing over coleslaw and stir well, adding more if needed.

Yields: 8 servings

Crispy Carrot & Radish Salad

This colorful salad is a perfect example of how you can turn even simple ingredients into something special!

5	medium carrots	5
¾ cup	sliced radishes	175 mL
¾ cup	chopped coriander leaves (cilantro)	175 mL
3 tbsp.	finely chopped red onion	45 mL
3 tbsp.	mayonnaise	45 mL
2 tsp.	lemon juice	10 mL
½ tsp.	prepared horseradish	2 mL
⅛ tsp.	salt	0.5 mL
⅛ tsp.	pepper	0.5 mL
	pinch of sugar	
3 drops	hot pepper sauce	3 drops

1. Pare and shred carrots. In a large bowl, toss carrots with radishes, coriander and onion.
2. In a small bowl, combine mayonnaise, lemon juice, horseradish, salt, pepper, sugar and hot pepper sauce.
3. Add to carrot salad and toss. Cover and refrigerate for 3 hours.

Yields: 8 servings

Pictured on page 51.

Marinated Carrot Salad

2 lbs.	carrots, sliced	1 kg
1	large Spanish onion, thinly sliced	1
1	large green pepper, sliced	1
10 oz.	can tomato soup	284 mL
1 cup	white sugar	250 mL
½ cup	cooking oil	125 mL
¾ cup	vinegar	175 mL
1 tsp.	salt	5 mL
1 tsp.	pepper	5 mL

1. Cook carrots until tender-crisp (do not overcook) and drain. Add onion and green pepper and set aside.
2. Combine the soup, sugar, oil, vinegar and seasonings in a small pot. Boil, stirring to dissolve the sugar. Pour over vegetables and cook on low heat for 2-4 minutes.
3. Cool salad and store in the refrigerator. Allow to marinate at least overnight before using.

Yields: 6-8 servings

Variation: Place hot salad in sterilized jars, and seal. Store in a cool place; it will keep for up to a year.

Overnight Vegetable Salad

This salad will keep for several days stored in a covered container in the refrigerator.

2 cups	fresh OR frozen steamed green peas	500 mL
2 cups	cooked green beans, 1" (2 cm) lengths	500 mL
1 cup	cooked fresh OR frozen corn	250 mL
1	medium onion, finely chopped	1
¾ cup	finely chopped celery	175 mL
2 tbsp.	chopped pimientos	30 mL

White Wine Vinegar Dressing:

¾ cup	sugar	175 mL
½ cup	vegetable oil	125 mL
½ cup	white wine vinegar	125 mL
½ tsp.	salt	2 mL
½ tsp.	pepper	2 mL

1. In a large bowl, combine peas, beans, corn, onion, celery and pimientos.
2. In a saucepan, combine dressing ingredients; heat and stir until sugar dissolves.
3. Pour dressing over the vegetables. Cover and refrigerate overnight.

Yields: 10-12 servings

There are more accidents in the kitchen . . .

Than in any other room in the house . . .

And husbands have to eat them . . .

Italian Vegetable Salad

Herbed Italian Dressing:

1 cup	vegetable oil	250 mL
⅔ cup	lemon juice	150 mL
½ cup	water	125 mL
½ cup	sugar	125 mL
2 tsp.	salt	10 mL
½ tsp.	pepper	2 mL
1 tsp.	dried oregano	5 mL
1	head cauliflower	1
4	medium carrots, cut in 2" (5 cm) strips	4
4	stalks celery, cut in 1" (2 cm) strips	4
½ cup	whole stuffed olives	125 mL

1. Combine the oil, lemon, water, sugar, salt, pepper and oregano and bring to a boil. Add vegetables; simmer for 5 minutes.
2. Add olives, put salad in a bowl and chill overnight. Drain before serving.

Yields: 6-8 servings

Sauerkraut Salad

This tangy salad will keep for a long time in the refrigerator.

Sweet & Sour Vinegar Dressing:

1¼ cups	white sugar	300 mL
½ cup	water	125 mL
½ cup	vinegar	125 mL
½ cup	vegetable oil	125 mL
4 cups	drained sauerkraut	1 L
1	medium onion, cut in rings	1
1 cup	diced celery	250 mL
1	green pepper, chopped	1
1	red pepper, chopped	1

1. In a small saucepan, bring dressing ingredients to a boil and cool.
2. Place vegetables in a large bowl. Pour dressing over vegetables. Cover and refrigerate for 24 hours; drain and serve.

Yields: 10 servings

Serve with potato salad and grilled sausages.

In The Sauce

(Sauces, Dips, Jams & Pickles)

Ranch Topping

Here is a topping as limitless as a prairie sky! When we get "culinary" brain waves and are stuck with the "dressing-up" part, we most often refer to our "Ranch Topping". I never use sour cream on my baked potatoes – always this topping recipe, it has a delightful flavor and drapes over the potatoes beautifully; no need to pass butter or extra salt and pepper. It is also a wonderful salad dressing for fresh cucumbers, onions, radishes or cauliflower and can be used as a vegetable dip. This is our best and so simple and easy to prepare.

¾ cup	plain yogurt*	175 mL
½ cup	mayonnaise*	125 mL
1 tsp.	sugar	5 mL
½ tsp.	salt	2 mL
½ tsp.	coarse-ground pepper	2 mL
1 tbsp.	chopped green onion	15 mL
1 tbsp.	chopped, fresh dillweed	15 mL

1. Mix all ingredients well with a wire whisk. Refrigerate.

Yields: 1½ cups (375 mL)

* To make a low-fat or no-fat topping, use low-fat or no-fat yogurt and mayonnaise.

Yogurt Mayonnaise Sauce

Use this tasty sauce or the Garlic Yogurt Sauce on all the pita recipes or over sliced cucumbers, as a potato topping or a dip.

½ cup	plain yogurt	125 mL
¼ cup	mayonnaise	60 mL
1 tsp.	sugar	5 mL

1. Mix all ingredients well and refrigerate until ready to use.

Yields: ¾ cup (175 mL) sauce

Garlic–Yogurt Sauce

1 cup	plain yogurt	250 mL
2	small garlic cloves, crushed	2
	salt and pepper to taste	

1. Combine all ingredients and refrigerate until ready to use.

Dilled Yogurt-Garlic Sauce

This is the most versatile sauce recipe you will ever find. Good with cold or warm vegetables, use it also as a dip or as a baked potato topping. Drop a teaspoonful of sauce in any vegetable soup or stew, or try it as a salad dressing.

1 cup	plain yogurt	250 mL
1 cup	sour cream	250 mL
2 tbsp.	mayonnaise	30 mL
2	garlic cloves, minced	2
1 tbsp.	chopped dillweed	15 mL
1 tsp.	sugar	5 mL
¼ tsp.	coarse pepper	1 mL
½ tsp.	salt	2 mL
½ tsp.	prepared herb and spice combination (e.g., Mrs. Dash)	5 mL

1. Blend all ingredients thoroughly with a wire whisk. Refrigerate. Will keep for 2 weeks.
2. If you use this as topping or dip, use as is. For a thinner consistency add a small amount of water.
3. If added to hot dishes, do not boil after sauce is added.

Yields: 2 cups (500 mL)

Mustard-Yogurt Dip

Marvelously tasty – you will be asked for this dip recipe again and again. It can be used as a salad dressing; served on the side with ham or beef; spooned over baked potatoes. This is also wonderful dip for all kinds of vegetables.

1 cup	plain yogurt*	250 mL
2 tbsp.	horseradish mustard	30 mL
2 tsp.	honey	10 mL
¼ tsp.	salt	1 mL

1. Combine all ingredients and refrigerate. Will keep refrigerated for 2 weeks.

Yields: 1 cup (250 mL)

* To make a low-calorie dip use low-fat or no-fat yogurt.

Famous Barrier Dill Sauce

This sauce can be used for many dishes. Pour over hard-boiled or poached eggs for breakfast or use on any type of fish dish; vegetables like cauliflower, broccoli, carrots or green beans; baked potatoes or French omelets.

⅓ cup	butter	75 mL
¾ cup	mayonnaise	75 mL
1	egg, beaten	1
¼ cup	lemon juice	60 mL
1 tbsp.	chicken soup base	15 mL
2 tbsp.	minced dillweed, fresh OR frozen	30 mL
¼ cup	water	60 mL
1 tbsp.	sugar	15 mL
	salt to taste (optional)	

1. Melt butter in small saucepan, add mayonnaise, beaten egg, lemon juice, chicken soup base, water, sugar and dill.
2. Over low heat, stirring continuously with a wire whip, bring sauce to a gentle boil until thickened. Add salt if you desire.

Yields: 1½ cups (375 mL)

Variation: If fresh or frozen dill is not available, use chopped, fresh cilantro.

Cheese Sauce

This sauce will keep in a closed container in the refrigerator forever and you can use it on practically anything.

1 cup	evaporated milk* OR light cream	250 mL
1½ cups	grated Cheddar cheese	375 mL
1 tsp.	salt	5 mL
¼ tsp.	paprika	2 mL
¼ tsp.	celery salt	2 mL
	few grains cayenne pepper	

1. Scald milk or cream. Stir in the rest of the ingredients.
2. Cook sauce over low heat, stirring constantly until smooth.

Yields: 2 cups (500 mL)

* If you are going to keep this sauce on hand for a long time – use the evaporated milk instead of the cream.

Easy Cheese Sauce

This tasty simple sauce adds interest to broccoli; cauliflower, etc.

1 cup	mayonnaise	250 ml
½ cup	milk	125 mL
½ cup	grated Cheddar cheese	125 mL
½ tsp.	paprika	2 mL

1. In a small saucepan, blend together all ingredients and heat, stirring constantly.

Yields: 1½ cups (375 mL)

Quick Herbed Tomato Sauce

Italian flavorings add zest to a commercial sauce to give you a quick and easy sauce for any pasta or rice dish. You can use this recipe whenever tomato sauce is called for, including pizzas or with ground beef.

14 oz.	can tomato sauce	398 mL
½ tsp.	crushed dried basil	2 mL
½ tsp.	crushed dried oregano	2 mL
⅛ tsp.	ground ginger	0.5 mL
1 cup	water	250 mL

1. In a small saucepan, combine all ingredients. Boil for 5 minutes.

Yields: 2½ cups (625 mL)

Sweet & Sour Pineapple Sauce

We make this sauce in large amounts and keep it in the refrigerator. Omit the cornstarch if you want to store it. Ideal over meatballs Oriental style, baked ham, short ribs, chicken breasts or shrimp. A sure shot!

1 tbsp.	butter	15 mL
¼ cup	finely chopped green pepper	60 mL
¼ cup	finely chopped red pepper	60 mL
⅓ cup	finely chopped onion	75 mL
1	garlic clove, minced	1
19 oz.	can pineapple tidbits	540 mL
⅓ cup	apple cider vinegar	75 mL
2 tbsp.	soy sauce	30 mL
2 tbsp.	honey	30 mL
¼ tsp.	salt	1 mL
2 tbsp.	cornstarch	30 mL
¼ cup	cold water	60 mL

1. In a medium saucepan, heat butter and sauté peppers, onion and garlic.
2. Add all other ingredients, except cornstarch and water, and cook 3 minutes.
3. Add cornstarch to cold water; mix to a thin paste. Add to sauce; cook and stir until thickened.

Yields: 3 cups (750 mL)

Mustard Gravy

May be used for fish dishes or ham, pork chops or green beans.

1 cup	chicken stock	250 mL
1 cup	milk	250 mL
¼ cup	dry mustard	60 mL
¼ cup	all-purpose flour	60 mL
½ cup	vinegar	125 mL
1 tsp.	salt	5 mL
1 tsp.	celery seed	5 mL
⅓ cup	honey	75 mL

1. Bring chicken stock to a boil. Add milk.
2. Combine mustard, flour, vinegar, salt and celery seed.
3. Add seasonings to chicken stock and milk mixture. Bring to a boil; simmer 5 minutes. Stir in honey.

Yields: 2½ cups (625 mL)

Keeps refrigerated 4-5 days.

The Best Dill Pickles

For 2 quarts (2 L):

2 qts.	dill-sized cucumbers	2 L
2	heads of dill	2
2	garlic cloves	2
2½ tbsp.	pickling salt	37 mL
2½ tbsp.	sugar	37 mL
1 cup	vinegar	250 mL
pinch	alum	pinch

1. Fill sterilized jars with clean cucumbers and dill. Add a clove of garlic to each jar.
2. Combine the remaining ingredients and use half of them for each quart (liter).
3. Pour in boiling water to within ½" (1.3 cm) of top and seal.

Yields: 2 quarts (2 L)

Barb's Marinated Beets

My friend Barb gave this recipe to me many years ago. I have never tasted better beets. You can make as many jars as you have beets. They will keep a year in a cool dark place. Pickled beets taste delicious with all kinds of meat dishes or as an accompaniment to sandwiches or pita bread.

2 cups	vinegar	500 mL
3 cups	sugar	750 mL
2 tsp.	mixed pickling spice, tied in a cheesecloth	10 mL

1. Wash and cook beets. Do not overcook; they should still be firm. Cool beets; peel and slice.
2. Place beets in sterilized jars.
3. Combine brine ingredients and boil 2 minutes. Remove pickling spice. Pour liquid over beets. Seal jars if you are storing beets for a long time.
4. Let beets marinate a few days before serving.
5. Drain and serve.

Yields: enough brine for 3 quarts (3 L) of beets.

Wild West's Best (Grilled Meats & Vegetables)

Orange-Kiwi Sauce

This sauce may be used as a dessert all by itself, but it tastes most delicious on pancakes. It's thick, fruity and visually very attractive. We've never had leftovers, but this sauce should keep, refrigerated for 3-4 days.

2	large oranges	2
2	kiwi fruit	2
½ cup	orange juice	125 mL
2 tbsp.	lemon juice	30 mL
2 tbsp.	honey	30 mL

1. Peel oranges, cut in halves and slice halves thinly; repeat with kiwis.
2. In a small saucepan, combine orange juice, lemon juice and honey; bring to a boil.
3. Add the fruit and simmer 2-3 minutes. Cool.

Yields: 2 cups (500 mL)

Pictured on page 17.

Rhubarb Sauce

What's a summer without a dish of ice cream topped with a yummy rhubarb sauce? This is also delicious on a slice of pound cake. Make lots, use it warm or cold in the spring of the year and freeze in small portions for later.

4 cups	chopped fresh rhubarb	1 L
1 cup	white sugar	250 mL
1 cup	orange juice	250 mL
dash	salt	dash

1. Combine all ingredients in a large saucepan. Cook over medium heat for 15-20 minutes, stirring occasionally, until rhubarb is soft.
2. Cool the sauce. Add more sugar if desired, depending on the sweetness you prefer.

Yields: 3 cups (750 mL)

This recipe can be doubled or tripled nicely.

Rodeo & Powwow
   activities

A Very Special Rhubarb Jam

5 cups	chopped rhubarb	1.25 L
1 cup	sugar	250 mL
½	orange with rind, chopped very finely	½
3 cups	sugar	750 mL
3 oz.	pkg. strawberry gelatin	85 g
3 tbsp.	liquid fruit pectin (1/2 pouch)	45 mL

1. Mix first 3 ingredients and let stand overnight.
2. In the morning, add the sugar to the rhubarb mixture and bring to a boil. Boil 10 minutes. Remove from heat.
3. Stir in gelatin powder and pectin; mix well.
4. Put jam in sterilized jars and seal.

Yields: 6 x 8 oz. (250 mL) jars

Pictured on page 17.

Freezer Raspberry Jam

This jam has a year-round fresh-fruit flavor.

2 cups	mashed raspberries	500 mL
4 cups	sugar	1 L
2 tbsp.	lemon juice	30 mL
½ cup	liquid pectin	125 mL

1. Wash, mash and measure raspberries.
2. Mix in the sugar.
3. Combine lemon juice and liquid pectin.
4. Stir into fruit mixture and continue stirring for 3 minutes.
5. Ladle into sterilized 8 oz. (250 mL) jars* and seal.
6. Allow to set at room temperature. Store in the freezer.

Yields: 5 x 8 oz. (250 mL) jars

   * I use good clean plastic containers and they work well.

Freezer Strawberry Jam

1¾ cups	crushed strawberries	425 mL
4 cups	sugar	1 L
2 tbsp.	lemon juice	30 mL
½ cup	liquid pectin	125 mL

1. Wash, stem and crush strawberries.
2. Mix in the sugar.
3. Combine lemon juice and liquid pectin.
4. Stir into fruit mixture and continue stirring for 3 minutes.
5. Ladle into sterilized jars* and seal.
4. Allow to set at room temperature. Store in freezer.

Yields: about 5 x 8 oz. (250 mL) jars

* I use good clean plastic containers and they work well!

Carrot-Pineapple Marmalade

2	medium oranges, untreated*	2
1	lemon, untreated*	1
14 oz.	can crushed pineapple	398 mL
1 cup	syrup from pineapple	250 mL
2 cups	cooked, shredded carrots	500 mL
1 tsp.	grated fresh ginger	5 mL
7 cups	sugar	1.75 L
2 x 3 oz.	liquid fruit pectin (2 pouches)	2 x 90 mL

1. Peel oranges and lemon; cut peel in thin, 1" (2.5 cm) long strips.
2. Cook orange and lemon peel in a small amount of boiling water until tender, about 15 minutes. Drain.
3. Drain pineapple, reserving 1 cup (250 mL) syrup.
4. Dice orange and lemon pulp; combine with drained pineapple and remaining ingredients, except pectin. Mix well.
5. Place fruit in preserve kettle; bring to a boil. Boil and stir for 7 minutes.
6. Remove marmalade from heat and add pectin. Skim and stir 1 minute.
7. Pour into hot sterilized jars; seal.

Yields: about 8 cups (2 L)

* Untreated (organic) fruit has no chemicals on the skin.

Zucchini Marmalade

6 cups	peeled, grated zucchini	1.5 L
6 cups	sugar	1.5 L
1 cup	crushed pineapple	250 mL
½ cup	lemon juice OR 1 lemon, chopped	125 mL
1	orange with rind*, chopped	1
½	grapefruit with rind*, chopped	½
2 x 3 oz.	pkgs. apricot gelatin	2 x 85 g

1. In a large saucepan, combine all ingredients, except gelatin.
2. Boil hard for 10 minutes; stir in the apricot gelatin.
3. Remove marmalade from heat, pour into sterilized jars and seal.

Yields: about 8 cups (2 L)

* Use organic or unsprayed oranges and grapefruit for the best marmalade.

Punches Western Style

Creeping Whiskey Punch

Great flavor, but be careful – this one creeps up behind you and knocks you out . . .

3 cups	orange juice, chilled	750 mL
3 cups	pineapple juice, chilled	750 mL
1½ cups	lemon juice, chilled	375 mL
1 cup	lime juice, chilled	250 mL
1 cup	light rum	250 mL
1 cup	rye whiskey	250 mL
½ cup	sugar	125 mL
	ice cubes	

1. Combine all the ingredients, except the ice, in a punch bowl; blend until the sugar is dissolved.
2. Float plenty of ice cubes on top.

Yields: 20, 4-oz. (125 mL) servings

Horse Thieves' Celebration Punch

3 x 26 oz.	bottles of sauterne wine, chilled	3 x 750 mL
2 qt.	bottle ginger ale	2 L
1	lemon, washed and sliced thinly	1
	a few sprigs of mint	
	ice cubes	

1. Combine the wine and ginger ale in a large punch bowl.
2. Float lemon slices and sprigs of mint on the top. Add ice cubes to keep chilled.

Yields: 22-24 servings

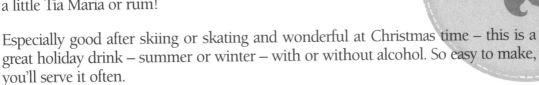

Cowhand's Pick-Me-Up

A delicious year-round beverage. This tastes good first thing in the morning, in between meals or around the campfire in the evening, with a little Tia Maria or rum!

Especially good after skiing or skating and wonderful at Christmas time – this is a great holiday drink – summer or winter – with or without alcohol. So easy to make, you'll serve it often.

3¾ oz.	instant vanilla pudding mix	106 g
⅓ cup	sugar	75 mL
1 tsp.	vanilla	5 mL
6 cups	milk*	1.5 L
2	eggs, separated	2
	Tia Maria OR rum (optional)	
	nutmeg	

1. In a large mixing bowl, beat together pudding mix, sugar, vanilla, milk and egg yolks.
2. Beat egg whites until stiff. Carefully fold into milk mixture. Chill thoroughly.
3. Pour into glasses and add an ounce of Tia Maria or rum if you wish. Top with a dash of nutmeg.

Yields: 8 cups (2 L)

*If you desire a thinner consistency, add more milk.

Sign in a Wisconsin Saloon:

He is not drunk . . . who from the floor
Can rise again and drink once more
But he is drunk . . . who prostrate lies
And cannot drink and cannot rise.

Anonymous

Rhubarb Sizzle Fizzle

Two nips of this will make you bite your ears off!

3 cups	chopped rhubarb, fresh OR frozen	750 mL
1 cup	water	250 mL
½ cup	sugar	125 mL
1 cup	apple juice	250 mL
6 oz.	frozen pink lemonade concentrate, thawed	178 mL
26 oz.	vodka	750 mL
2 qt.	bottle lemon lime soda	2 L

1. In a medium saucepan, combine rhubarb, water and sugar; bring to a boil.
2. Reduce heat; cover and simmer for 5 minutes, or until rhubarb is tender. Cool for about 30 minutes.
3. In a food processor or blender, purée mixture, half at a time.
4. Stir in apple juice and lemonade concentrate.
5. Pour into a freezer container; cover and freeze until firm.
6. Let stand at room temperature for 45 minutes before serving.
7. For individual servings, scoop ⅓ cup (75 mL) of rhubarb mixture into a glass, add 2 oz. (60 mL) of vodka and fill with soda. To serve a group, place all of the mixture in a large pitcher or punch bowl; add vodka, soda and stir. Serve immediately.

Yields: about 10 servings

Variation: This also makes a tart and tangy nonalcoholic punch – just omit the vodka.

Corn Likker
Described by Irvin S. Cobb

It smells like gangrene starting in a mildewed silo,

*It tastes like the wrath to come
and when you absorb a deep swig of it –
you have all the sensations of having
swallowed a lighted kerosene lamp.*

*A sudden, violent jolt of it has been known
to stop the victim's watch,
snap his suspenders and
crack his glass eye right across.*

Red Dynamite Punch

Guaranteed to blow your head off

2 lbs.	diced rhubarb (7-8 cups [1.75-2 L])	1 kg
3 cups	water	750 mL
6 oz.	can frozen lemonade	178 mL
2 x 6 oz.	cans water	356 mL
½ cup	sugar	125 mL
2 qts.	bottle ginger ale	2 L
26 oz.	gin	750 mL

1. Simmer the rhubarb in the 3 cups (450 mL) of water until tender, about 5 minutes. Strain and keep juice, discard pulp.
2. Chill the juice (approximately 4 cups [1 L]).
3. To chilled juice, add frozen lemonade, 2 cans of water and sugar. Just before serving, add ginger ale and gin.

Yields: approximately 10 cups (2.5 L)

Variation: To defuse this punch, just leave out the gin – great flavor and no hangover.

The Mixologist
by Mark Twain

The cheapest and easiest way to become an influential man, and be looked up to by the community at large in the old West, was to stand behind a bar, wear a cluster-diamond pin, and sell whiskey.

The Hangin' Hide Posts these Rules

✳ "Pocketing" at meals strictly forbidden

✳ Gentlemen are expected to wash out of doors and find their own water.

✳ Lodgers must furnish their own straw.

✳ Beds on barroom floor reserved for regular customers.

✳ Persons sleeping in the bar are requested not to take off their boots.

✳ Lodgers inside arise at 5 a.m.; in the barn at 6 a.m.

✳ Each man sweeps up his own bed.

✳ No quartz taken at bar

✳ No fighting allowed at the table.

Anyone violating the above rules will be shot.

April 28, 1895, by order of the Sheriff

The Ways of the Old Western Saloons

Food bad – water worse – cooking THE worst.

A guest, objecting to dirty linen was told;

Twenty-six gents have used this towel afore you, stranger,

But you're the first to complain.

Sign on an old Arizona Saloon
Anonymous

Greens & Not So Green . . .
(Vegetables)

Stuffed Baked Potatoes

3	large baking potatoes (1 lb. [500 g])	3
1 tsp.	vegetable oil (optional)	5 mL
½ cup	sliced green onions	125 mL
½ cup	butter OR margarine (divided)	125 mL
½ cup	light cream	125 mL
½ cup	sour cream	125 mL
1 tsp.	salt	5 mL
½ tsp.	white pepper	2 mL
1 cup	shredded Cheddar cheese	250 mL
	paprika	

1. Rub potatoes with oil if desired; pierce skins with a fork. Bake at 400°F (200°C) for 1 hour and 20 minutes, or until tender.
2. Allow potatoes to cool to the touch.
3. Cut potatoes in half lengthwise; carefully scoop out pulp, leaving a thin shell.
4. Place pulp in a large bowl.
5. Sauté onions in ¼ cup (60 mL) butter until tender. Add to potato pulp with light cream, sour cream, salt and pepper. Beat until smooth. Fold in cheese.
6. Stuff potato shells and place in a 9 x 13" (23 x 33 cm) baking pan.
7. Melt remaining butter; drizzle over the potatoes. Sprinkle with paprika.
8. Bake at 350°F (180°C) for 20-30 minutes, or until heated through.

Yields: 6 servings

Optional: Potatoes may be stuffed ahead of time and refrigerated or frozen. Allow additional time for reheating.

Pictured on page 139.

Cheese Potato Puff

12	medium potatoes, peeled (about 5 lbs. [2.2 kg])	12
1 tsp.	salt, divided	5 mL
¾ cup	butter OR margarine	175 mL
2 cups	shredded Cheddar cheese	500 mL
1 cup	milk	250 mL
2	eggs, beaten	2
	fresh OR dried chives, optional	

Greens & Not So Green . . .

Cheese Potato Puff continued

1. Place potatoes in a large pot; cover with water. Add ½ tsp. (2 mL) salt; cook until tender.
2. Drain; mash potatoes until smooth.
3. In a saucepan, over medium heat, combine and cook butter, cheese, milk and remaining salt, stirring until smooth.
4. Stir into potatoes; fold in eggs.
5. Pour potato mixture into a greased shallow 3-quart (3 L) baking dish. Bake, uncovered, until puffy and golden brown. Sprinkle with chives if desired.

Yields: 8-10 servings.

Optional: Casserole may be covered and refrigerated overnight. Allow to stand at room temperature for 30 minutes before baking.

This is excellent with Honeyed Ham, page 162, and Sweet and Sour Red Cabbage, page 113.

Garlic Potato Patties

Do you ever wonder what to do with those leftover mashed potatoes? This dish has everybody asking for more and no second guessing about leftovers!

2 cups	mashed potatoes	500 mL
½ cup	all-purpose flour	125 mL
	salt and pepper	
3	slices bacon, diced	3
½ cup	chopped onions	125 mL
2	garlic cloves, minced	2
	flour for dusting	
	vegetable oil	

1. Mix mashed potatoes and flour. Blend well; add salt and pepper to taste.
2. Fry diced bacon until cooked, but not crisp. Add onion and garlic; sauté until onion is translucent.
3. Add to mashed potato and mix well. Use your hands, coated with flour, to form patties.
4. Dust patties with flour and fry patties on both sides in a lightly oiled skillet on medium heat until lightly browned.

Yields: 4-6 servings

These are delicious with smokies, fried fish and steam-fried cabbage.

Western Roundup Potatoes

Simple to make, this is delicious with barbecued steaks, fish or shish kabobs.

2 lbs.	frozen hash browns	1 kg
1 cup	diced onions	250 mL
10 oz.	cream of chicken OR mushroom soup	284 mL
1 cup	grated sharp cheese	250 mL
½ cup	butter OR margarine	125 mL
1 cup	sour cream	250 mL
	salt and pepper to taste	
	cornflake crumbs (optional)	

1. Thaw potatoes for 30 minutes.
2. Combine all ingredients, except crumbs, and pour into a 9 x 13" (23 x 33 cm) baking pan. Top with corn flake crumbs, if using.
3. Bake at 350°F (180°C) for 1 hour.

Yields: 8-10 servings

Turnip Potatoes

From Ron, a good friend, this recipe elevates the turnip to "gourmet status".

4 cups	mashed potatoes (see below)	1 L
2 cups	mashed yellow turnip (see below)	500 mL
¼ cup	half and half cream	60 mL
5	slices Canadian (back) bacon, diced	5
1	medium onion, chopped	1
1	garlic clove, minced	1
1 tsp.	EACH sugar and salt	5 ml
	nutmeg	

1. Cook potatoes and turnips in separate saucepans; drain well. Mash potatoes with the cream; mash drained turnips.
2. Dice bacon and fry until crisp. Remove bacon from pan. Discard half the bacon fat and sauté the chopped onion and garlic in the remaining fat.
3. Whip all ingredients together, mixing well. The turnip-potato mash should be soft and creamy; add more cream if necessary. Sprinkle with nutmeg.
4. The success of this dish relies on the right ratio of the turnip and potatoes. Make sure the ratio is ⅓ turnip to ⅔ potatoes.

Yields: 4-6 servings
Serve with Grilled Buffalo Steaks, page 116, and Roasted Green Chilies, page 87.

Pictured on page 157.

Vegetable Rice Pilaf

This savory side dish has been a hit for many years; serve it with any grilled entrée.

1 tbsp.	butter OR margarine	15 mL
¾ cup	uncooked, long-grain rice	175 mL
¼ tsp.	dried crushed basil	1 mL
2 cups	chicken stock	500 mL
¾ cup	frozen peas and carrots	175 mL
¼ cup	chopped sweet red pepper	60 mL
	fresh basil leaves for garnish	

1. In a 2-quart (2 L) saucepan over medium-high heat, melt butter; add rice and basil and cook until rice is browned, stirring constantly.
2. Stir in chicken stock. Heat to boiling; reduce heat to low; cover and cook for 10 minutes. Add peas, carrots and red pepper.
3. Cover; cook for 10 minutes, or until rice is tender and liquid is absorbed. Garnish with fresh basil if desired.

Yields: 4 servings

Rice Loaf

A very simple yet impressive dish, invert on an oval plate and cut in 1" (2.5 cm) slices. Spoon mushroom or tomato sauce over slices. You may fry leftover slices in very hot oil on both sides until crisp. Serve for lunch with a salad.

2	garlic cloves, minced	2
1	onion, chopped	1
2	celery stalks, chopped	2
2 tbsp.	butter	30 mL
2 cups	cooked rice	500 mL
½ cup	Parmesan cheese, grated	125 mL
½ tsp.	curry powder	2 mL
2	eggs, beaten	2
	salt and pepper to taste	

1. Preheat oven to 350°F (180°C).
2. In a medium frying pan, melt butter; add garlic, onion and celery and sauté gently for a few minutes.
3. Mix together all ingredients.
4. Spoon the rice mixture into an ovenproof bread pan or 1-quart (1 L) baking dish and bake for 30-40 minutes, until it is firmly set.

Yields: 6-8 servings

Creamed Mushrooms

We very often use mushrooms we pick ourselves in our back yard. A few hundred acres of forest bring forth a large variety of wild mushrooms. Many Saskatchewan settlers in the early 1900s came from Ukraine and brought this recipe with them. I don't think any Ukrainian household celebrates Christmas without this dish.

1½ lbs.	fresh mushrooms, wild OR cultured	750 g
1	large onion, chopped	1
	butter	
½ cup	chicken stock	125 mL
½ cup	heavy cream	125 mL
	cornstarch	
	salt and pepper to taste	
1 tsp.	dillweed OR 1 tbsp. chopped fresh dill	5 mL

1. Clean and slice mushrooms.
2. Melt butter and sauté onion in butter. Add chicken stock and mushrooms; cover and cook for 15 minutes. Wild mushrooms may require a slightly longer cooking period.
3. Add cream and heat through; do not boil. Add cornstarch dissolved in a little cold water. Cook on low until thickened. Add salt and pepper to taste.
4. When ready to serve, stir in the dillweed.

Yields: 6-8 servings

This dish is wonderful with steaks or any type of wild meat. It's a classic served over perogies or wide noodles.

Mushrooms & Sour Cream

Try this Ukrainian specialty to serve either cultivated or wild species of mushrooms. Sour cream adds a delightful, piquant flavor to this dish, a wonderful accompaniment to steaks with small new potatoes, wide noodles or perogies.

1	small onion, chopped	1
1	garlic clove, crushed	1
2 tbsp.	butter	30 mL
1 lb.	mushrooms, cleaned and sliced	500 g
2 tbsp.	cornstarch OR flour	30 mL
1 cup	sour cream	250 mL
	salt and pepper to taste	
1 tsp.	chopped fresh dill OR ½ tsp. (2 mL) dried dillweed	5 mL

Mushrooms & Sour Cream

continued

1. In a large frying pan, melt butter and sauté onion and garlic. Add mushrooms; cover and cook 15 minutes. Wild mushrooms may require a longer cooking period.
2. Blend the cornstarch with some of the sour cream to make a smooth paste; stir in the remaining cream.
3. Add sour cream to the mushrooms. Cook, stirring, until mixture gently boils. Add salt and pepper to taste.
4. When ready to serve, stir in the dillweed.

Yields: 6 servings

Wild mushrooms . . . to eat . . .
or not to eat

Wild mushroom picking at our Ranch always makes for an interesting story.

Two young couples from Germany decided to use the first sunny day after a rainy stretch to go mushroom picking. After thorough interrogation from the rest of the guests, to determine if their knowledge of mushrooms was sufficient to ensure that the flight back home would not be in a horizontal position, they enthusiastically set off . . . armed with two large pails and a can of mosquito spray!

Two hours later they returned with beaming smiles and full pails.

The happy faces of the rest of the guests froze into worried frowns after I promised to make a delicious creamed mushroom dish out of their bounty. All of a sudden no one was really fond of mushrooms. So I decided to take matters into my own hands and suggested an ingenious plan. Make up the mushroom dish and serve part of it to our young mushroom experts for lunch; if they still appeared for supper we would ALL eat the mushrooms. All afternoon, they were very solicitously asked about their welfare and every trip to the house with the little moon was registered!

Needless to say, the mushrooms were delicious and all around the table were happy and contented smiles. The mushroom pickers turned into HEROES!!! See the picture on page 158.

Company Cauliflower

When time is short and you want something delicious, try this recipe!

1	head of cauliflower	1
½-¾ cup	sour cream	125-175 mL
¼ cup	milk	60 mL
	salt and pepper to taste	
¾ cup	grated Cheddar cheese	175 mL
1 cup	bread cubes OR croûtons	250 mL

1. Clean cauliflower and break into bite-sized pieces.
2. Cook for 8-10 minutes. Drain well.
3. Put cauliflower into a buttered 2-quart (2 L) casserole. Combine the sour cream with the milk, salt, pepper and grated cheese. Pour over the cauliflower.
4. Top with croûtons. Bake at 375°F (190°C) for ½ hour.

Yields: 4 servings

Creamy Cauliflower Casserole

Tired of cauliflower and cheese sauce? This one is different and delicious! It will bring you rave reviews

1	head of cauliflower, cut into florets	1
½ cup	sour cream	125 mL
½ cup	mayonnaise	125 mL
¾ cup	grated Cheddar cheese	175 mL
½ cup	water	125 mL
¼ tsp.	salt	1 mL
½ cup	croûtons	125 mL

1. In a saucepan, cook cauliflower 6-8 minutes. Drain well.
2. With a wire whisk, blend together sour cream, mayonnaise, cheese, water and salt.
3. Place cauliflower in a greased 2-quart (2 L) casserole and cover evenly with the sauce mixture. Top with croûtons.
4. Bake at 375°F (190°C) for 45 minutes.

Yields: 4-5 servings

Greens & Not So Green . . .

Grilled Mixed Vegetables

Grilling gives vegetables fabulous flavor. It's also perfect for hot days – no need to heat up the stove.

2	cobs corn	2
2	small sweet red peppers	2
2	small green peppers	2
6	small onions	6
3	mild chilies, cut in half	3
	salt and pepper to taste	

1. Cut cobs of corn into 3 pieces each; cut pepper into large pieces; peel onions but leave whole.
2. Blanch vegetables for 2 minutes, drain, spray with oil and grill over low heat, 2 minutes on each side.
3. Salt and pepper to taste.

Yields: 6 servings

Serve alongside Ranch Steak, page 146.

Hint: If your barbecue has a grill with widely spaced bars, use a barbecue grill basket for grilling vegetables.

Pictured on page 87.

Roasted Green Chilies

For those who like it "hot"!

2	chilies per serving	2

1. Wash chilies thoroughly. Place on hot grill 5 minutes on each side or until skin is blistered and fairly black.
2. Remove from heat, cool slightly and gently scrape off outer skin.

Serve at once on top of steaks.

Note: Chili peppers come in over 200 varieties. Jalapeño peppers are one of the mildest and most popular varieties and they range from hot to very hot – even peppers from the same bush vary considerably. Experiment to find your favorites.

Pictured on page 87.

Grilled Corn

When you have the barbecue going for your meat dish, what is easier than to throw on the vegetables too? Grilled corn has wonderful flavor and aroma.

use 1 ear of corn per person.

1. Trim silk from the husks, but leave husks intact.
2. Soak corn in cold water for 1 hour.
3. Preheat grill. Remove corn from water, drain and place on hot grill.
4. Grill corn for 10 minutes; turn corn and grill another 10 minutes. Spray with water if husks appear too dry.
5. Remove corn from grill; remove husks; brush with melted butter and sprinkle with salt and pepper.

Variation: Try a sprinkle of cayenne and/or chili powder if you want a hotter flavor.

Pictured on page 139.

Corny Casserole

This vegetable casserole complements any meat dish.

14 oz.	can creamed corn*	398 mL
2	eggs, beaten	2
1 cup	shredded Cheddar cheese	250 mL
2 tbsp.	all-purpose flour	30 mL
2 tbsp.	sugar	30 mL
¼ tsp.	salt	1 mL
1 tbsp.	chopped fresh dill	15 mL
	pepper to taste	
	dill sprigs for garnish	

1. Combine all ingredients except dill sprigs and pour into a well-greased 1-quart (1 L) casserole.
2. Bake 45 minutes at 350°F (180°C) or longer if you double the recipe.
   3. Garnish with a few sprigs of dill.

Yields: *4-6*

* Fresh corn may be used: add ⅓ cup (75 mL) of half-and-half cream to 1 cup (250 mL) corn kernels.

Swiss Chard Surprise

Ever wondered what to do with those big white stalks? Use the tangy leaves for another dish and use only the stalks for our Swiss Chard Surprise. This is my most asked-about vegetable dish.

2 cups	chicken stock	500 mL
1 lb.	Swiss chard stalks, cut in 3" (7 cm) pieces OR 2* stalks per person	500 g
⅓ lb.	feta cheese, crumbled	150 g
1 cup	whipping cream	250 mL
1	egg, separated	1
	salt and pepper to taste	

Topping:

2 tbsp.	vegetable oil	30 mL
2 tbsp.	bread crumbs	30 mL

1. In a large saucepan, bring chicken stock to a boil, add stalk pieces and cook 10 minutes. Drain stalks and rinse under cold water.
2. In a blender, purée the feta cheese with 3 tbsp. (45 mL) of the cream. Set aside.
3. Whip the rest of the cream with the egg white until foamy but not stiff. Add the egg yolk and feta cheese; blend well.
4. In a 2-quart (2 L) greased casserole, arrange stalks. Pour cream mixture evenly over stalks, sprinkle with salt and pepper.
5. Combine topping ingredients and sprinkle over casserole.
6. Bake at 350°F (180°C) for 15 minutes, or until golden brown.

Yields: 4 servings

* 1-2 depending on size

Greens & Not So Green . . .

Campfire Beans

This old west classic is a real crowd pleaser! Trouble with the digestion? Well, go on a long wild gallop across the Prairie – after that the beans won't bother you!!!

1 lb.	dry pinto beans	500 g
6 cups	water	1.5 L
½ lb.	bacon, cut in 1" (2.5 cm) pieces	250 g
1	large onion, diced	1
¼ cup	dark molasses	60 mL
½ tsp.	dry mustard	2 mL
½ tsp.	black pepper	2 mL
¼ tsp.	cayenne pepper	1 mL
	salt and pepper to taste	

1. Soak beans overnight in water to cover generously.
2. Drain beans, discarding bean liquid.
3. Add 6 cups (1.5 L) of fresh water to beans.
4. In a large roasting pan, combine all the ingredients. Cook at 300°F (150°C) for 2-2½ hours, or until beans are tender.
5. Season with salt and pepper to taste.

Yields: 8 servings

Serve alongside Buffalo Steak Burgers, page 117, or regular burgers on a Kaiser bun or bannock.

Note: If you don't want to follow the above advice – you may want to add some dried kelp or kombu strips to the beans, it helps digestion and wards off intestinal gas. Discard after cooking.

Pictured on page 87.

Cowboy Bean Casserole

This fast and easy dish is an excellent companion to hamburgers or hot dogs. It can be prepared ahead of time and reheated when needed. It also freezes well.

1 cup	diced ham	250 mL
2 tbsp.	butter OR margarine	30 mL
1	garlic clove, minced	1
19 oz.	can baked beans	540 mL
19 oz.	can red kidney beans	540 mL
14 oz.	can lima beans, drained	398 mL
1 tbsp.	brown sugar	15 mL
½ cup	ketchup	125 mL
3 tbsp.	vinegar	45 mL
	salt and pepper to taste	
1	medium onion, sliced	1

1. In a small frying pan, melt butter and sauté ham.
2. Combine garlic, beans, ham, sugar, ketchup, vinegar and seasonings.
3. Pour into a greased 2-quart (2 L) casserole and top with onion slices. Cover and bake at 350°F (180°C) for 50 minutes.

Yields: 6 servings

Baked Cabbage Wedges

Showy and scrumptious. This dish will elevate the lowly cabbage to company fare. Delicious with any grilled or barbecued meat, even the most sophisticated world travellers found this to be a wonderful way to serve cabbage.

1	medium cabbage	1
1 cup	sour cream	250 mL
2	garlic cloves, minced	2
2	eggs, slightly beaten	2
½ tsp.	thyme, fresh OR dried	2 mL
¼ tsp.	nutmeg	1 mL
1	large tomato, chopped	1
½ tsp.	salt	2 mL

Topping:

2 tbsp.	vegetable oil	30 mL
½ cup	grated Cheddar cheese	125 mL
2 tbsp.	bread crumbs	30 mL

1. Cut cabbage in wedges, leaving part of core on each wedge. In a large saucepan, cook cabbage wedges 10 minutes; drain well.
2. Place cabbage wedges in a greased 9 x 13" (23 x 33 cm) pan.
3. With a wire whisk, blend together sour cream, garlic, eggs, thyme, nutmeg, tomato and salt. Pour evenly over cabbage.
4. Combine topping ingredients and sprinkle over cabbage. Bake 30-40 minutes at 400°F (200°C).

Yields: 8 servings

Sweet & Sour Red Cabbage ★

A truly old European dish that found it's way across the ocean many, many years ago. Europeans are still delighted by it and it has many North American enthusiasts. Our goose hunting guests from the U.S. enjoy it with fried or roasted goose. Also excellent with ham, chicken, turkey or any wild meat, this dish has a lovely color and superb flavor. You may want to adjust the "sweet and sour" balance to taste.

1	small head of red cabbage, shredded	1
1	large sour apple, peeled and cubed	1
3	slices bacon, cut in large pieces	3
1 tsp.	whole cloves	5 mL
½ cup	water	125 mL
½ cup	apple cider vinegar	125 mL
1½ tsp.	salt	7 mL
½ cup	sugar	125 mL
1 tbsp.	cornstarch	15 mL

1. In a large saucepan, combine all the ingredients except cornstarch and bring to a boil. Simmer for 45 minutes.
2. Stir cornstarch into a little cold water to make a thin paste. Add to cabbage mixture; cook and stir until thickened.

Yields: 6-8 servings

*There are great builders
In all walks of life . . .
But the greatest of them
operate in the kitchens . . .
where they build health
and happiness for generations!!!*

Greens & Not So Green . . .   113

Homemade Sauerkraut

If you have been disappointed in the quality and taste of commercial sauerkraut, try your hand at making your own. This is very mild and delicious! You may want to make enough for a whole year. It is very easy to make, very healthy and more flavorful and less expensive then commercial varieties. It will turn a sauerkraut hater into a "Sauerkraut Fan"! All the sauerkraut we use at the ranch is homemade.

| 5 | medium-sized firm heads of cabbage | 5 |
| 1 cup | coarse pickling salt | 250 mL |

1. Thoroughly wash a 4-gallon (15 L) earthenware crock.
2. Remove outer cabbage leaves; wash and put aside. Wash and weigh all the cabbage; it should total 20-25 lbs. (9-11 kg). The measurements given here are not very exact, since it matters little if the crock is ¾ full or completely full.
3. Slice 1 cabbage with a slicer or shredder, by hand or with a kitchen machine.
4. Put the cabbage in the crock and mix with 1½ tbsp. (22 mL) salt. Pack down well. Repeat layering until all heads have been used.
5. Place the large cabbage leaves on top.
6. Fold several layers of cheesecloth, about 1 yard (1 m), to fit diameter of crock; place on cabbage.
7. Place a round wooden board or an upside-down plate over the cheesecloth and weigh it down with a well-washed rock, about 10-12 lbs. (4.5-5 kg), or other similar weight. The weight should be heavy enough to make the brine show over the cloth.
8. Cover and let stand in a cool place for 5-6 weeks.
9. Check once a week. If foam shows on top of the board or dinner plate, remove rock, cheesecloth and board or plate. Remove foam. Rinse plate, rock and cheesecloth well and replace.
10. Repeat whenever foam develops.
11. Taste sauerkraut after 5 weeks. If kraut is not thoroughly cured, let it sit another week.
12. Place sauerkraut in plastic bags and freeze, or process in sterile jars in a hot water bath for 20 minutes.

Yields: 12-14 quarts (11-13 L)

Bucks, Ducks & Things that Swim

(Fish & Wild Game)

Grilled Buffalo Steaks

Wild west flavor tamed with red wine and spiced with garlic – hearty and delicious. Try the marinade with beef also.

4-5	medium buffalo steaks	4-5

Red Wine Garlic Marinade:

1½ cups	red dry wine	375 mL
½ cup	chopped onion	125 mL
4	garlic cloves, minced	4
2 tsp.	Worcestershire sauce	10 mL
1 tsp.	dried thyme	5 mL
1 tsp.	coarse pepper	5 mL
½ cup	cooking oil	125 mL

1. Tenderize steaks with a meat mallet. Combine all remaining ingredients in a plastic bag, large enough to hold all the steaks; shake vigorously.
2. Place steaks in the bag and shake to coat meat. Seal and refrigerate overnight, turning steaks occasionally.
3. Preheat grill. Remove steaks from marinade and pat dry.
4. Grill steaks about 10 minutes on each side for medium doneness, longer for thicker steaks.

Yields: 4-5 servings

Don't know much about cooking buffalo meat???

There is no such thing as tough buffalo meat, only improperly instructed cooks. Just keep in mind "low and slow", the oven temperature should never be higher than 275°F (140°C). A slow cooker or crock pot are ideal for this type of meat.

Buffalo has often been called the original health food. Buffalo meat is significantly higher in protein, yet lower in fat, cholesterol and calories than most other meats.

And it tastes good, too! Some folks say it tastes like beef – hearty, sweet and rich with no gamey taste at all.

Buffalo is often available in specialty stores in cities or you can enquire about a buffalo farm near you.

Barrier Buffalo Steaks

2 lbs.	buffalo steak, cut 1" (2.5 cm) thick	1 kg
	flour	
	salt and pepper	
	vegetable oil for frying	
1	medium onion, chopped	1
1 cup	heavy cream	250 mL
½ lb.	fresh mushrooms, cut in large pieces	250 g

1. Coat steak in the flour; add salt and pepper to both sides.
2. Heat oil in a large skillet and brown onions.
3. Remove onions and brown floured steak on both sides.
4. Return onion to the skillet and add the cream and mushrooms.
5. Cover the pan and cook on top of stove at very low heat, or bake in the oven at 325°F (160°C), for 2½ hours. Add more water if necessary.

Yields: 3-4 servings

Buffalo Steak Burgers

1½ lbs.	ground buffalo meat	750 g
1	medium onion, minced	1
1	garlic clove, minced	1
¼ cup	ketchup	60 mL
6	slices bacon, diced	6
½ cup	fine bread crumbs	125 mL
1	egg, slightly beaten	1
1 tsp.	salt	5 mL
	dash of coarse pepper	
	cheese	
	tomatoes	
	onions	

1. Combine all ingredients well, except cheese, tomatoes and onions. Form meat mixture into patties.
2. Preheat grill.
3. Grill patties over medium heat, 10 minutes on each side.
4. Top burgers with cheese, sliced tomatoes and onions, if desired.

Yields: 6-8 patties

Serve with Campfire Beans, page 110, a real Western meal!

Great Buffalo Stew

So good . . . And so easy!!!

4 oz.	diced bacon	125 g
2 lbs.	buffalo stew meat	1 kg
2 cups	chopped celery	500 mL
2 cups	chopped onion	500 mL
2 cups	chopped green pepper	500 mL
1 tbsp.	chopped parsley	15 mL
3-4 cups	water, divided	750 mL-1 L
1	large bay leaf	1
1½ tsp.	salt	7 mL
½ tsp.	pepper	2 mL
2 cups	diced potatoes	500 mL
2 tbsp.	cornstarch	30 mL
2 tbsp.	water	30 mL

1. In a large skillet or electric frying pan, fry bacon until crispy and remove from pan.
2. Brown buffalo meat in bacon fat; remove from pan.
3. Sauté the celery, onion, pepper and parsley 2-3 minutes in the remaining fat.
4. Return the meat to the pan and add 2 cups (500 mL) water, bay leaf and seasonings. Stir up brown bits from the bottom of the pan.
5. Cover the pan and simmer until the meat is tender, about 2 hours.
6. Stir in crisp bacon, potatoes and 1 cup (250 mL) of water (more if needed).
7. When the potatoes are cooked, blend cornstarch into water. Add to stew and cook until juices are thickened. Serve at once!

Yields: 4-6 servings

This makes a hearty meal with grilled garlic bread, or Trailside Corn Bread, page 39.

Pictured on page 121.

Corn-Muffin-Topped Buffalo Pie

1½ lbs.	ground buffalo	750 g
1 tbsp.	chopped onion	15 mL
2 tbsp.	butter OR margarine	30 mL
1 cup	beef stock	250 mL
1 tsp.	chopped parsley	5 mL
⅛ tsp.	pepper	0.5 mL
1 tsp.	salt	5 mL
2 tbsp.	Worcestershire sauce	30 mL

Corn Bread Topping:

1½ cups	yellow cornmeal	375 mL
2 tbsp.	flour	30 mL
1 tsp.	baking soda	5 mL
½ tsp.	salt	2 mL
¾ cup	buttermilk OR sour milk	175 mL
2	eggs, beaten	2

1. In a heavy skillet, heat butter and sauté meat and onions.
2. Stir in beef stock, parsley, pepper, salt and Worcestershire sauce.
3. Spread meat mixture in a 2-quart (2 L) casserole, leaving a 2" (5 cm) space at the top.
4. To prepare corn bread topping, combine all dry ingredients; add milk and eggs, and stir until smooth. Press carefully on top of the casserole. Bake at 325°F (160°C) for 30 minutes.

Yields: 5-6 servings

Moose Balls

(No! not what you think!)

1½ cups	ground moose meat	375 mL
½ cup	dry bread crumbs	125 mL
1	egg, beaten	1
1	garlic clove, crushed	1
1½ tsp.	salt	7 mL
	pepper to taste	
½ cup	grated sharp Cheddar cheese	125 mL
1 tsp.	ground ginger	5 mL

Herbed Tomato Sauce:

14 oz.	can tomato sauce	98 mL
½ tsp.	crushed dried basil	2 mL
½ tsp.	crushed dried oregano	2 mL
⅛ tsp.	ground ginger	0.5 mL
1 cup	water	250 mL

1. Combine meat, bread crumbs, egg, garlic, salt and pepper.
2. Mix cheese with ginger and press into tiny balls, about the size of a small olive. Set aside.
3. Form meatballs the size of golf balls and press cheese balls into the center, enclosing the cheese balls completely in the meat mixture. Brown meatballs on all sides over medium heat.
4. Place meatballs in a casserole.
5. Combine all sauce ingredients in a small saucepan. Boil for 5 minutes. Pour over moose balls.
6. Bake at 350°F (180°C) for 30-40 minutes.

Yields: 4-6 servings

Wild Game (Buffalo)
Great Buffalo Stew, page 118
German-Style Fusilli Salad, page 46
Trailside Corn Bread, page 39

Bucks, Ducks & Things That Swim

Venison Roast

This roast tastes wonderful hot or cold, tender and juicy with only the tiniest hint of wild meat. Does the taste of wild meat ever bother you? Then try this method. (Moose or Elk may also be used.)

Garlic Wine Marinade:

6 cups	dry white wine	1.5 L
1 cup	wine vinegar	250 mL
1 cup	chopped green onion	250 mL
4	garlic cloves, crushed	4
1 tsp.	salt	5 mL
2 tsp.	coarse pepper	10 mL
1 tbsp.	dried basil	15 mL
2	bay leaves	2
2-3 lbs.	venison, moose OR elk roast	1 kg

1. Combine all marinade ingredients and bring to a boil. Simmer 5 minutes to blend spices.
2. Place the roast in a nonmetal bowl and pour the marinade over the meat. Cover tightly and refrigerate 3 days, turning meat now and then.
3. Remove the roast from the marinade and place in a roasting pan; cover. Roast at 325°F (160°C) for 2½ hours, or until meat is tender.
4. Let stand 10 minutes. Cut into thin slices.

Yields: 6-8 servings

Serve with the Mustard Yogurt Dip on page 81, with fried potatoes or piled on a crusty bun. Don't forget a green salad.

Buffalo near
Barrier Chaparral ranch

Smoked Ukrainian Sausage

My husband George is of Ukrainian ancestry and also an avid hunter so combine those 2 factors and you get recipes like this. He has been making sausage out of wild meat for 25 years and has honed and perfected this recipe to an unforgettable treat. It tastes heavenly warm – just coming out of the smoker, but it is equally delicious cold on buns or sandwiches Also try this prairie treat brushed with barbecue sauce and cooked on a grill. It's surprisingly simple to make and he loves the accolades our guests lavish on him.

20 lbs.	wild meat	9 kg
5 lbs.	pork trim* (75% fat)	2.2 kg

Seasonings:

5 cups	ice cold water	1.25 L
2 cups	soy protein concentrate (use only if desired for filler)	500 mL
10 tbsp.	coarse salt	150 mL
3 tbsp.	sugar	45 mL
5 tsp.	prague powder #1**	25 mL
2½ tbsp.	coarse black pepper	37 mL
12	large fresh garlic cloves	12
2 tbsp.	marjoram	30 mL
1 tbsp.	ground coriander	15 mL
1 tsp.	dried savory	5 mL
1 tsp.	cayenne pepper	5 mL

1. *Grinding and Trimming:* Trim excess fat off meat. Remove and discard blood clots, bone, sinews, cords, etc. Grind all the lean meat through a ⅜" (9 mm) grinder plate and all the fat meat through a ⅛" (3 mm) plate. Alternately, take the meat to a local locker plant or butcher and have him do the grinding and add the pork trim.
2. In an electric blender, blend the ice water and all the seasoning ingredients. Place ground meat in a very large mixing bowl, add the blended spices and mix until evenly distributed.
3. *Stuffing the Sausage:* Sausage should be stuffed into a large-size hog casing, then place it on smokehouse sticks, spaced 1" (2.5 cm) apart. Permit sausage to dry.
4. *Dry the sausage as follows:* When stuffing the sausage, it normally is hung on the sausage sticks in the room where you are working. By the time you are finished stuffing the sausage, much of it already is dry. To finish drying, you may put sausage in a preheated smokehouse at 130°F (55°C) with dampers wide open for about 1 hour, or until casings are dry and starting to take on a brown color.

5. *Smoking:* Sausage is placed in a preheated smokehouse or you may use an old gutted steel refrigerator with a hot plate placed at the bottom. Heat the smoker to 130°F (55°C), with dampers or door partly open. Maintain this temperature until the casings are dry. Close door or dampers and gradually increase temperature of smokehouse to 165-175°F (70-80°C).

   Apply heavy smoke by setting a container of nonresin sawdust on one of the burners and refill as necessary. Keep sausage in smoker for 3-4 hours, until sausage reaches an internal temperature of 152°F (75°C).

   Remove sausage from smokehouse and douse it with cold tap water until the internal temperature is reduced to 110°F (55°C). Allow the sausage to hang at room temperature for about 30 minutes, or until the desired bloom (color and shine) is obtained.

Yields: about 20 lbs. (9 kg) of sausage

At this point, the sausage is fully cooked and can be eaten out of hand. Sausage may be kept in the refrigerator or frozen in plastic bags for up to 4 months. Sausage can be used in many recipes and in many different ways; as sandwich meat or in soups. It is excellent with any type of bean dish; cooked over a campfire on the trail or brushed with barbecue sauce and grilled. Cut sausage in 1" (2.5 cm) chunks and thread on skewers alternately with a vegetable for an easy shish kabob; it grills to perfection. Throughout this book you will find dozens of uses for smoked sausage – have fun with it; give it a try!!!

* Pork trim is the fatty trim from pork. As indicated, it is 75% fat and is used to add tenderness and flavor to the sausage.

** Prague powder #1 is a basic cure that is used to cure all meats that require smoking. The definition "Prague powder #1" is well known to all butchers across North America. It can be obtained at any locker plant, butcher shop or any retailer specializing in sausage preparation. Prague powder #1 is actually a small amount of sodium nitrite on a salt carrier.

North American Indian Pemmican

This is an ancient Indian recipe given to me by an elderly Native woman, at one of the Pow Wows we attended.

Use moose, elk, or deer meat
Cut meat very thinly into strips long enough to hang over a rack.
Oil a wooden dowel and hang meat strips over the dowel. Make a smudge to keep insects off.
Put meat out in the sun every day, near the smudge, until the meat is thoroughly dried and so brittle it cracks. This takes a few days.
Put the meat into a cloth and pound until it is powdery.
Work small amounts of bacon dripping into the meat until the meat can be formed into balls. Dried Saskatoon berries may be worked in for better flavor. This meat mixture will keep indefinitely; sun-dried meat never spoils. Try this very rewarding ancient Indian method.

Dried Saskatoon Berries

Scrub two window screens and spread 2-3 layers of cheesecloth on the screen. Spread Saskatoon berries on the cloth. Cover with 2-3 layers of cheesecloth, top with a second screen and dry in the sun. When quite dry, place the berries in a cloth bag to store. Use for pemmican or in muffins.

Bucks, Ducks & Things That Swim

Trapper's Rabbit Stew

If you've never tried rabbit, this dish will show you how tasty and delicious it is!

1	rabbit, cut into serving pieces	1
4 cups	boiling water	1 L
½ cup	white wine	125 mL
2 tbsp.	olive oil	30 mL
½ tsp.	dried sage	2 mL
½ tsp.	dried thyme	2 mL
2	large potatoes, sliced	2
1	large onion, diced	1
1 cup	whole-kernel corn	250 mL
2	large carrots, sliced	2
2	garlic cloves, minced	2
1	mild green chili, chopped	1
	chopped cilantro for garnish	

1. Brown rabbit on all sides in a heavy skillet.
2. Place meat in a roasting pan; add remaining ingredients, except cilantro.
3. Cover pan and bake at 325°F (160°C) for 1½ hours.
4. Garnish with cilantro and serve with Indian Bannock, page 34.

Yields: 4-6 servings

Partridge or Prairie Chicken with a Chinese Touch

This makes an excellent meal on the trail or while out hunting. In the fall we just have to sit on our porch and in no time – out walks the main ingredients of our supper, two and three at a time. Partridge are not just wonderfully tasty but also very interesting to watch. The proud strutting and show-off behavior of the male grouse, its drumming mating dance, adds to the mystery of the wild. The meat is extraordinarily tasty with hardly any gamy flavor. This recipe will delight any hunter and the accolades will be endless.

2	grouse breasts	2
3 tbsp.	vegetable oil	45 mL
½ cup	bean sprouts	125 mL
½ cup	sliced mushrooms	125 mL
1 cup	sliced celery	250 mL
½ cup	frozen green peas	125 mL
¼ cup	water	60 mL
1 tbsp.	soy sauce	15 mL
½ tsp.	salt	2 mL
½ cup	slivered, toasted almonds	125 mL
	parsley for garnish	

1. Cut each grouse breast in half. In a skillet, heat oil and fry breasts until almost done, about 3 minutes each side.
2. Add all other ingredients, except almonds and parsley, and cook with cover on, for 3-5 minutes.
3. Add almonds, garnish with parsley.

Yields: 4-6 servings

Biscuits will complete the meal.

Wild Goose Breasts à la Barrier Chaparral

4	large duck OR goose breasts	4
¼ cup	vinegar	60 mL
	coarsely ground steak spice	
	paprika	
¾ cup	flour	175 mL
1 tbsp.	dried parsley	15 mL
2	eggs, beaten	2
1 cup	buttermilk	250 mL
1½ cups	crushed crackers	250-375 mL
	vegetable oil for frying	
2	garlic cloves, crushed	2
	Parmesan cheese	

1. Soak goose breasts in cold water and vinegar for 1 hour. Drain breasts and rinse.
2. Remove membranes from breasts and slice each breast lengthwise twice. This will give you 3 slices from each breast side, 12 thin slices in total.
3. Tenderize meat with a meat mallet and sprinkle steak spice and paprika on each slice.
4. Combine flour and parsley and roll meat slices in flour mixture.
5. Combine eggs and buttermilk and dip meat slices into egg mixture, then in crushed cracker crumbs.
6. Heat ¼-½" (1-1.3 cm) of oil in a frying pan on medium heat; add garlic and fry meat quickly on both sides. Sprinkle with Parmesan on 1 side only.

Yields: 6-8 servings

Serve with spaghetti and tomato sauce, sprinkled with Parmesan cheese.

Goose or Duck Breasts — Swiss Style

If your taste buds cannot get accustomed to the unique taste of wild waterfowl, try this recipe; you will be converted forever!

Hunting and eating go together. After all, a wild game dinner with family or friends is the warmest and best way to relay hunting stories in detail.

8	duck breasts OR 6 goose breasts, cut in halves	8
	vegetable oil for frying	
2	carrots, sliced	2
2 cups	very finely chopped celery	500 mL
1 cup	very finely chopped onion	250 mL
½ cup	whipping cream	125 mL
1 cup	water	250 mL
1½ cups	beef stock	325 mL
1 tsp.	salt	5 mL
½ tsp.	sugar	2 mL
⅓ tsp.	coarse pepper	0.5 mL

1. Rinse breasts; pat dry.
2. Heat oil in a skillet and brown breasts quickly on both sides. Remove breasts from skillet and sauté celery and onions.
3. Arrange breasts in a roasting pan. Sprinkle carrots and sautéed celery and onions over meat.
4. With a wire whisk, stir together cream, water, beef stock, salt, sugar and pepper.
5. Pour over meat and vegetables.
6. Cover and bake at 325°F (160°C) for 1½-2 hours.

Yields: 8 servings

Serve with broad noodles, Marinated Carrot Salad, page 76, and top it off with Pineapple Cream Pie, page 184.

130 *Bucks, Ducks & Things That Swim*

Smoked Wild Goose Breasts

any quantity of goose breasts.

Brine:

1 cup	curing salt, such as Quik-Cure*	250 mL
3	garlic cloves, crushed	3
4 cups	water	1 L

1. Make enough brine, in the above ratio, to cover goose breasts.
2. Leave the breasts in the brine for 2 days, or until the cure penetrates the entire breast. By cutting into one of the breasts, you can determine how far the cure has penetrated by the change of color.
3. Remove breasts from brine and rinse thoroughly in cold water. Dry well with paper towel.
4. Put breasts on an oiled grill and place in preheated smoker or smoke house. (You can also use a covered barbecue as a smoker.)
5. Operate the smoker or barbecue at 145-155°F (63-63°C) for 1-1½ hours, to remove all moisture from the breasts.
6. Place hickory wood chips on the hot coals of the smoker or barbecue and increase heat to 170-180°F (77-82°C) for another 3-4 hours, or until the breasts are well cooked and take on a very dry appearance.
7. Remove goose breasts from the smoker and let cool. Use fresh or place in plastic freezer bags and freeze.

> **Cut goose breasts very thinly across the grain and serve as a special hors d'oeuvre on crackers. Great with a beer! Many guests have "gone wild" over this!!**

* The salt adds flavor and when used in adequate amounts acts as a mild preservative, inhibiting bacterial action.

Let's Become Fish "Poachers"

The most healthful cooking process for fish is poaching – no fats or oils are used. It gives you firm control over the flavors that you choose to impart to the fresh fish and you can poach any species of fish you catch.

The poaching process is simple. The liquid is the key. It ensures that the fish will not dry out, which commonly happens when baking, broiling or frying. The poaching liquid also determines the flavor the fish will absorb.

The cooking liquor you choose can be a simple vegetable broth or a more ambitious court bouillon. Here is a basic court bouillon.

Court Bouillon:

8 cups	water	2 L
2	carrots, cut in chunks	2
1	onion, chopped	1
3	lemon OR lime slices with seeds	3
8	peppercorns	8
pinch	tarragon	pinch
1 tbsp.	parsley	15 mL
1	bay leaf	1

1. Simmer all ingredients together for 45 minutes before adding fish. You will need a fish poacher, which is a 2' (60 cm) long covered roasting pan, with a rack to lower the fish into and raise it out of the bubbling broth. A regular roaster, skillet or saucepan can be used, provided it is covered and large enough to hold the fish or fish pieces while immersed. Cheesecloth can be used for the rack.
2. Leave the skin on – it holds the fish together and the juices in. You can remove the skin before serving.
3. If you are poaching a whole fish, cook for about 10 minutes per inch (2.5 cm) of thickness (measured across the thickest part of the fish's back). Poaching is forgiving, so a few minutes more will not overcook your fish. It is also a good idea to leave the head on while cooking as it enhances flavor. Remove the skin and head before serving.

Try the Famous Barrier Dill Sauce, on page 82. Serve poached fish hot or cold, with lemon, flavored butter or your favorite sauce. The leftover fish works well in salads or chowders. Also save the cooking liquid, strain, seal and freeze for later use as stock in soups or chowders.

Scott's Special Fish-Fry

A few summers ago we had a group of "executive" guests at the Ranch. My son Scott arrived, just back from a very successful fishing trip on the Churchill River. With his stubbed chin and rumpled clothes he hardly solicited much admiration from these "would be" cowboys, just newly clad in pinching cowboy boots, tight jeans and shiny new belt buckles. However, Scott promised them a seafood treat they'd never forget. My "Queen of the kitchen" status was instantly reduced to "spectator" status. As we waited, delicious smells emanated from the open kitchen window. A short while later Scott proudly emerged with a large, basket full of delectable deep-fried fish morsels. After only one round of that heavenly basket; he was instantly heralded as the "fishing hero" of Canada. The mmhs – ahs and ohs didn't stop until 5 pounds of fish were enthusiastically "tasted" away. Since then all our repeat guests ask for this dish and even though Scott wrote it all down for me – it's never ever tasted as good as on that day. This fish recipe may also be used as an appetizer.

2-3 lbs.	Saskatchewan walleye*	1-1.5 kg
1 cup	all-purpose flour	250 mL
½ cup	whole-wheat flour	125 mL
1 tsp.	baking powder	5 mL
1 tbsp.	lemon pepper	15 mL
½ tsp.	garlic powder	2 mL
1 tsp.	salt	5 mL
1 tsp.	dried sage	5 mL
12 oz.	can beer (not Labbatt's) OR 7-Up	341 mL
2 cups	vegetable oil for deep frying	500 mL

1. Cut fish in 1-1½" (2.5-4 cm) pieces.
2. Combine flours, baking powder, lemon pepper, garlic powder, salt and sage; add beer or 7-Up and beat with an electric mixer. Let stand for 10 minutes.
3. Heat oil in a deep fryer or electric skillet to 375°F (190°C).
4. Roll fish pieces in batter and cook for 5-10 minutes, until golden brown.
5. Place fried fish on several layers of paper towels to absorb excess oil; keep fish warm. Continue until all fish is cooked.
6. Sprinkle fish with lemon juice and serve with tartar sauce.

Yields: 6-8 servings

Every fisherman's favorite, enjoy this with Vegetable Rice Pilaf, page 103, Green Pea Salad, page 72. Creamy Rice Pudding page 181, to round off this fisherman's dream meal!

* Only boned fish may be used in this recipe.

Catch of the Day à la Stroganoff

This is an unusual way to serve fish. If you are tired of fried fish try this gourmet-style dish. Dress it up for company fare.

2 tbsp.	vegetable oil	30 mL
½ lb.	fresh mushrooms, sliced	250 g
1 tbsp.	finely chopped red pepper	15 mL
4	green onions, cut in 1" (2.5 cm) pieces	4
1 lb.	any type of warm water fish, cut in fillets	500 g
¼ cup	dry white wine	60 mL
⅓ cup	sour cream	75 mL

1. In a large frying pan, heat oil; add mushrooms, red pepper and green onions and sauté for 2 minutes. Remove and set aside.
2. Sauté fish over medium heat for 3 minutes on each side. Remove to a platter, cover and keep warm.
3. Add wine and sour cream to frying pan; stir until hot. Add sautéed mushrooms, onions and red peppers. Stir gently for 1 minute; do not boil. Salt and pepper to taste. Pour mushroom mixture over fish.

Yields: 2-3 servings

Salmon Barbecue

1½ lb.	whole Pacific salmon	750 g
2 tbsp.	lemon juice	30 mL
3 tbsp.	olive oil	45 mL
	freshly ground coarse pepper	
	chopped fresh herbs to garnish (optional)	

1. Cut salmon in half lengthwise, along the backbone. Mix together the lemon juice and oil; season lightly with pepper.
2. Rub oil mixture into the fish and let it stand 1 hour.
3. Sprinkle fresh herbs on cut side of fish; wrap each half in 2 layers of heavy-duty foil. Barbecue, skin side up, 4-5 minutes over medium heat; turn and cook another 4-5 minutes.
4. Let fish rest 5-10 minutes. Transfer to a warm serving platter and garnish with more herbs and lemon slices.

Yields: 5-6 servings

Serve with Dilled Cucumber Salad, page 73, on the side.

Barbecued Fish Fillets in Foil

Easy and fast to prepare, this is colorful, moist and flavorful. It can be enjoyed at any camping or picnic facility, with any type of fish.

Tangy Seafood Sauce:

1 cup	ketchup OR chili sauce	250 mL
2 tbsp.	horseradish (not creamy horseradish sauce)	30 mL
2 tbsp.	lemon juice	30 mL
	pepper and salt to taste	
2 tsp.	Worcestershire sauce	10 mL
	Tabasco to taste	
6	fish fillets	6
12	scallops, diced	12
1	large onion, diced	1

1. Combine all sauce ingredients.
2. Cut 6 foil pieces, each large enough to enclose a fillet; grease lightly with oil.
3. Place each fillet on foil; sprinkle with scallops (2 scallops for each fillet) and onions. Cover generously with seafood sauce. Close foil packets tightly and let stand 1 hour.
4. Preheat grill. Cook packets over medium heat 10-15 minutes, depending on thickness of fillets. Do not turn. You can cook these in an oven at 350°F (180°C) for 15-20 minutes.

Yields: 6 servings; makes 1 cup (250 mL) of sauce

Serve with Cucumber Slaw, page 74, and Vegetable Rice Pilaf, page 103.

Pictured on page 139.

Catch of the Day — in Aspic

This recipe is not as complicated as it sounds and the results are well worth the effort – it is spectacular!!! Any type of lake fish is suitable. A most versatile dish, it is excellent as a side dish, for a buffet table, lunch, picnic or served with fried potatoes as a supper dish. It can be made up to 2 days ahead.

Fish:

1	medium onion, cut in large chunks	1
1	large carrot, sliced	1
1	celery stalk, sliced	1
2	sprigs of parsley, coarsely chopped	2
4	peppercorns	4
2	bay leaves	2
1½ tsp.	salt	7 mL
6	medium fish fillets	6

Aspic:

¼ cup	red pepper, in thin strips	60 mL
¼ cup	green pepper, in thin strips	60 mL
¼ cup	yellow pepper, in thin stirps	60 mL
½ cup	sliced thinly cucumber	125 mL
¼ cup	onion, sliced thinly	60 mL
½ cup	green peas, cooked	125 mL
3 tbsp.	unflavored gelatin (3 env.)	45 mL
¾ cup	cold water	175 mL
3¼ cups	vegetable-fish broth (add water if needed)	800 mL
¼ cup	red wine vinegar	60 mL
¼ cup	lemon juice	60 mL
1 tbsp.	sugar	15 mL
1½ tsp.	salt	7 mL
¼ tsp.	pepper	1 mL
	red and green pepper strips	
	mayonnaise for garnish (optional)	

Catch of the Day — in Aspic

continued

1. To prepare fish, put vegetables, parsley, peppercorns, and bay leaves into a 2-quart (2 L) Dutch oven; sprinkle with salt.
2. Place fish fillets on vegetable mixture; cover with boiling water and simmer until fish is tender, approximately 10-15 minutes. Do not permit it to boil.
3. Lift the fish out and cool. Pull fish apart just enough to remove bones. Strain vegetable broth and use liquid for aspic.
4. To prepare the aspic, first prepare the aspic vegetables.
5. Soften gelatin in cold water. Dissolve in boiling broth.
6. Add vinegar, lemon juice, sugar, salt and pepper to the dissolved gelatin.
7. Add vegetables to the gelatin mixture; mix carefully and let sit in the refrigerator for about 20 minutes, until starting to gel. Pour ½" (1.3 cm) of vegetable gelatin into an oiled bread pan, place fish on gelatin base and pour remaining gelatin over fish. Chill until firm, preferably overnight.
8. To serve, invert fish on an oval plate, decorate with red and green pepper strips and lots of mayonnaise, if desired.

Yields: 10-12 servings

Canned Fish

If you have an avid fisherman in your family and too many of those critters are littering your freezer, try canning them. You won't be sorry and may never buy a can of salmon again. You may use northern pike, walleye, perch, lake trout, whitefish, rainbow trout, brook trout.

For each quart (liter):

4 tbsp.	tomato soup* (NOT CREAMED)	60 mL
2 tbsp.	vegetable oil	30 mL
2 tbsp.	vinegar	30 mL
1 tsp.	salt	5 mL
	fish fillets	

1. Place all ingredients but the fish in the bottom of a sterilized 1-quart (1 L) jar.
2. Cut fillets into 2½-3" (6-7 cm) pieces. Pack fish into jars up to 1" (2.5 cm) from the top.
3. Seal jars and process for 3 hours in boiling water canner.

Note: Low-acid foods such as meat and fish must be processed at high temperatures in a pressure canner, or for long periods of time in boiling water (i.e., 3 hours).

Things That Swim
(Barbecued Fish & Seafood)

Barbecued Shrimp & Scallop Kabobs

Spicy Butter Baste:

½ cup	butter	125 mL
2 tbsp.	finely chopped onion	30 mL
1 tbsp.	Cajun OR Creole seasoning	15 mL
1 tsp.	hot pepper sauce	5 mL
1	garlic clove, minced	1

Kabobs:

18	large sea scallops (1 lb. [500 g])	18
12	large shelled shrimp, tails left on, deveined (¾ lb. [340 g])	12

1. Melt butter in a small heavy saucepan. Add onion, seasoning, hot pepper sauce and garlic; blend well. Place shrimp and scallops in a 2-quart (2 L) glass baking dish. Pour basting mixture over shrimp and scallops so they are coated. Let stand at room temperature for 30 minutes.
2. Heat grill. When ready to barbecue, oil grill rack.
3. Thread 3 scallops and 2 shrimp alternately on each of 6 metal skewers. Place kabobs on grill over medium heat, turning once and frequently brushing with the basting mixture until scallops are opaque, about 3-5 minutes.
4. Heat any remaining basting mixture to a boil and serve with kabobs.

Yields: 6 servings

Along the Barrier River

Bucks, Ducks & Things That Swim

Scalloping Kabobs

Here is a pleasant surprise for the barbecue season. No dish solicits more ahs and ohs than this one. This seafood grilling idea combines exciting flavors for succulent results.

9	slices bacon, halved across	9
18	large scallops (1 lb. [550g])	18
6	canned pineapple slices, 4 pieces each	6
12	large shrimp, shelled, tails left on (¾ lb. [340 g])	12

Seafood Barbecue Sauce:

3 tbsp.	vegetable oil	45 mL
2 tbsp.	chopped onion	30 mL
3 tbsp.	prepared tangy seafood sauce	45 mL
1 tsp.	hot pepper sauce	5 mL
1	garlic clove, crushed	1

1. Roll ½ slice bacon around each scallop.
2. Thread wrapped scallops, pineapple and shrimp alternately on 12-14" (30-35 cm) metal skewers, approximately 3 scallops and 2 shrimp on each skewer.
3. Place kabobs in a flat glass dish.
4. Combine all sauce ingredients and pour over kabobs. Let stand at room temperature for 45 minutes.
5. Preheat barbecue grill, then oil grill rack generously.*
6. Over medium heat, cook kabobs 3-5 minutes on each side, or until shrimp turn pink and scallops turn opaque. Brush frequently with the sauce.

Yields: 6 servings

* If you want to broil the kabobs in the oven, broil 4-6" (10-15 cm) from the heat, turning once. Brush with sauce.

Serve with buttered toasted biscuits.

Pictured on page 139.

Wild West's Best

to grill — or not to grill . . . (Meats)

Kicking Chicken Barbecue

A real winner at the ranch, this is unforgettable in many ways! Not just the chicken will be kicking!!!

| 1 | large chicken, cut into serving pieces OR | 1 |
| | 6 chicken legs with thighs | |

Kicking Lemon Marinade:

¾ cup	lemon juice	175 mL
5	garlic cloves	5
2	fresh jalapeño chilies, minced	2
½ tsp.	salt	2 mL
¼ tsp.	pepper	1 mL

1. Rinse chicken and pat dry.
2. In a blender, combine lemon juice, garlic, chilies, salt and pepper. Blend until smooth.
3. Pour marinade into a large plastic bag, add chicken pieces and marinate 2 hours in refrigerator, shaking the bag occasionally so the chicken gets well coated.
4. Preheat barbecue grill. Cook 20-30 minutes, turning frequently and basting with the marinade.

Yields: 6 servings

Serve with a pasta salad or potato salad to "calm" the palate. Cowboy Bean Casserole, page 111, and French bread are also a great options.

Have plenty of beverages handy!!!

Pictured on page 87.

Hints: *No more burnt barbecued chicken*

Partially cooking chicken in the microwave oven reduces grilling time and prevents flare-ups and burning.

Place chicken pieces in a microwaveable dish, cover with microwave-safe plastic wrap and cook 10 minutes, turning after 5 minutes.

Proceed with your favorite barbecue recipe.

Hill Dilly Chicken

Fast, easy and super delicious! Put together in 30 minutes and *voila* – wait for the compliments.

8-10	chicken pieces, skinned	8-10
	pepper	

Mushrooms & Sour Cream:

1½ lbs.	fresh mushrooms, wild OR cultured	750 g
1	large onion, chopped	1
	butter	
½ cup	chicken stock	125 mL
½ cup	heavy cream	125 mL
	cornstarch	
	salt and pepper to taste	
1 tsp.	dillweed OR 1 tbsp. (15 mL) chopped fresh dill	5 mL
1 tbsp.	lemon juice	15 mL
	paprika	

1. Place chicken in a single layer in a greased 9 x 13" (23 x 33 cm) baking pan. Sprinkle lightly with pepper.
2. Clean and slice mushrooms.
3. Melt butter and sauté onion. Add chicken stock and mushrooms; cover and cook for 15 minutes. Wild mushrooms may require a slightly longer cooking period.
4. Add cream, heat through, do not boil. Add cornstarch dissolved in a little cold water. Cook on low until thickened. Add salt and pepper to taste.
5. Remove sauce from the heat and stir in the dillweed and lemon juice. Pour over chicken pieces. Sprinkle with paprika.
6. Bake chicken, uncovered, at 350°F (180°C) for 1 hour, or until tender.

Yields: 6-8 servings

Serve with broad egg noodles and the Overnight Vegetable Salad on page 77. A German Apple Torte, page 171, will turn this into a Sunday feast!

Ranch Steak with Peppercorns & Zesty Barbecue Butter

This is an ideal way to serve steak to a rather large crowd. You may want to barbecue 2 pieces of meat if you are serving more than 10. This method is far easier than barbecuing a large number of individual steaks and the flavor is superb.

2½-3 lb.	sirloin steak, 3-5" (7-13 cm) thick	2.25-2.5 kg
2 tsp.	coarsely cracked garlic peppercorns*	10 mL

Zesty Barbecue Butter:

½ cup	butter, softened	125 mL
¼ cup	woodsmoke-flavor barbecue sauce	60 mL
1½ tsp.	minced parsley	7 mL
1	small garlic clove, crushed	1

1. Sprinkle the cracked garlic pepper evenly over the steak. Press in seasonings with fingertips. Refrigerate 5-6 hours.
2. Meanwhile, combine butter and remaining ingredients; beat until smooth. Place in a small bowl; set aside.
3. Preheat barbecue on high. Grill steak on both sides until almost black, about 5-8 minutes per side.
4. Turn grill on low heat and continue cooking for 10 minutes on each side. If you prefer a more rare steak 5-8 minutes each side will be sufficient. Remove steak from grill and wrap in 2 layers of heavy foil.
5. Allow steak to rest for 15 minutes. The steak will continue cooking in the foil.
6. Unwrap steak and cut into thin slices; steak slices will vary from well done on the outside to medium and rare toward the middle. Spoon meat juices over steak slices.
7. Pass around the Zesty Barbecue Butter.

Yields: approximately 6-7 servings

We serve this with Western Roundup Potatoes, page 102, and Grilled Mixed Vegetables, page 107, with Pumpkin Whip, page 186, for dessert.

* Garlic peppercorn blend is available in most supermarkets.

Barbecued Steaks

George's "Best in the West" steaks. According to our guests these are the best steaks they have ever eaten anywhere. But no guarantees . . . maybe it's the cook?

6	rib-eye steaks ¾-1" (2-2.5 cm) thick	6
	garlic powder	
	salt	
	high quality steak spice	

1. Pat the steaks dry. Sprinkle garlic powder, salt and steak spice on each side of steaks and rub spices in well.
2. Stack steaks on a plate and cover tightly with plastic wrap. Refrigerate 5 hours.
3. Preheat grill.
4. Sear steaks on high heat on both sides. Continue grilling over medium heat according to the degree of doneness that is desired, about 3-4 minutes for rare, 4-6 minutes for medium and 6-8 minutes for well-done.

Yields: 6 serving

This all-time favorite is best served with roasted Parmesan potatoes and Italian Vegetable Salad, page 78. A light cool dessert of ice cream and Rhubarb Sauce, page 89, will give the perfect finishing touch to a great meal.

Pictured on page 87.

Sauerbraten

This marinated pot roast is a traditional German meal. It gives an ordinary pot roast a deliciously different twist and is ideal for less tender cuts of meat. Give it a try!

3-4 lb.	beef roast	1.5-2 kg
	salt and pepper	
2	garlic cloves, slivered	2
1	medium onion, sliced	1

Marinade:

⅓ cup	wine vinegar	75 mL
4 cups	water	1 L
½	lemon, washed and sliced	½
6	whole peppercorns	6
2	bay leaves	2
4	whole cloves	4
2 tbsp.	tomato paste	30 mL
1 tbsp.	sugar	15 mL
1	carrot, thinly sliced	1
1 tbsp.	prepared mustard	15 mL

Gravy:

2 tbsp.	flour	30 mL
3 tbsp.	vegetable oil	45 mL
½ cup	sour cream	125 mL
1	medium onion, chopped	1
2 tsp.	sugar	10 mL

1. Rub beef with salt and pepper. Make an incision with the point of a sharp knife and insert garlic slivers. Place beef in a nonmetal bowl and cover with onion slices.
2. In a medium saucepan, combine all marinade ingredients and bring to a boil. Simmer 5 minutes to blend spices.
3. Pour marinade over meat. Cover tightly and refrigerate 24 hours, turning meat now and then.
4. Sauté chopped onions in oil in a large heavy Dutch oven, remove onions and set aside.
5. Drain meat from marinade, reserving the marinade. Pat meat dry with paper towels. Dust lightly with flour and brown meat on both sides in the Dutch oven.

Sauerbraten continued

6. Strain marinade.
7. Return sautéed onions and 3 cups (750 mL) of the strained marinade to the Dutch oven and roast the beef and onions for 3 hours at 325°F (160°C).
8. Place meat on a heated platter and make the gravy by adding a paste of water and 2 tbsp. (30 mL) flour to the pan juices. Stir over medium heat until smooth and thickened.
9. Blend sour cream, sugar and ¼ cup (60 mL) of strained, cold marinade. Add to to the gravy; heat through but do not boil.

Yields: 6-8 servings

Serve the gravy over thinly sliced sauerbraten and mashed potatoes. Sweet and Sour Red Cabbage, page 113, goes very well with this meat dish as does Creamy Cauliflower Casserole, page 106.

Prairie Oysters

Round-up time is Prairie Oyster time – in spring, when the branding is done and a bull becomes a steer! You may use any amount of oysters, generally 4-6 per person. For the squeamish, be assured, these taste very good and the meat is rich and tender.

> prairie oysters (bull testicles)
> water
> vinegar
> salt
> eggs
> milk
> bread crumbs
> garlic powder
> salt and pepper to taste
> vegetable oil for frying

1. Slit the sack; pull out oysters. Remove cords and soak oysters in a bowl of water, vinegar and salt for 2 hours.
2. Drain and rinse.
3. Combine egg and milk; roll oysters in egg mixture.
4. Combine bread crumbs, garlic powder, salt and pepper. Coat oysters in crumb mixture.
5. Fry oysters over medium heat, in plenty of oil, until browned and crisp. Drain on paper towels.

Fried potatoes are perfect with this dish.

Ranch Stew with Dumplings

Here is one of those recipes you throw together; turn on the slow-cooker and forget about it. Go out riding!

2 lbs.	beef, cut in bite-sized chunks	1 kg
¼ cup	all-purpose flour	60 mL
1 tbsp.	vegetable oil	15 mL
1 tbsp.	paprika	15 mL
1 tbsp.	salt	15 mL
1	green pepper, thinly sliced	1
2 cups	chopped tomatoes	500 mL
½ cup	water	125 mL
3	onions, sliced	3
1 tsp.	marjoram	5 mL
¼ tsp.	pepper	1 mL
1	garlic clove, minced	1
¼ cup	flour	60 mL
	crushed peppercorns (optional)	

1. Shake beef with ¼ cup (60 mL) flour to coat on all sides, brown in oil, add onions.
2. Combine the rest of the ingredients; add the beef and put in a slow cooker; cook 7 hours on low. If you don't own a slow cooker, simmer on low for 1½ hours or bake at 300°F for 3 hours.

Yields: *4-6 servings*

Serve with Dumplings (next page), Yogurt Cucumber Salad, page 73, and something you will never forget – Sex-is-Best-in-the-West Dessert, page 185.

May you always have that
special ingredient that gives life's stew its flavor!!

Dumplings:

1½ cups	all-purpose flour	375 mL
2 tsp.	baking powder	10 mL
¾ tsp.	salt	4 mL
3 tbsp.	shortening	45 mL
¾ cup	milk	175 mL

1. Sift together the flour, baking powder and salt.
2. Cut in the shortening. Stir in milk and mix only until blended.
3. Shape dough into approximately 8 dumplings and place gently on top of the stew. Cook uncovered for 10 minutes and cook covered for another 10 minutes.

Yields: 8 dumplings

Bonanza Chili

To be known to make you still spur your horse, even after you are not in the saddle any more!!!

1½ lbs.	ground beef	750 g
1½ cups	chopped onions	375 mL
1 cup	chopped green pepper	250 mL
2	garlic cloves, minced	2
19 oz.	can dark red kidney beans	540 mL
4	fresh tomatoes OR a 19 oz. (540 mL) can of tomatoes, cut up	4
10 oz.	can tomato sauce	284 mL
3 tsp.	chili powder	15 mL
½ tsp.	dried basil	2 mL
1 tsp.	salt	5 mL

1. In a large skillet, brown ground meat, onions, green pepper and garlic. Drain off fat.
2. Add all other ingredients, cover and cook 30 minutes.

Yields: 4-6 servings

Serve with toasted garlic bread. Add Strawberry Trifle, page 190, for dessert and you'll be in Bonanza Heaven!!

Wild West's Best

Texas Chili Beans

When you serve this, all you'll hear will be . . . Man . . . that's gooooood chili!!

1 lb.	ground beef	500 g
2	medium onions, chopped	2
19 oz.	can red kidney beans	540 mL
5½ oz.	can tomato paste	156 mL
1 cup	water	250 mL
½ cup	chopped green peppers	125 mL
1 tsp.	salt	5 mL
2 tsp.	chili powder	10 mL
1 tsp.	crushed dried red chilies	5 mL

1. In a large skillet, brown meat and onions.
2. Add all other ingredients and simmer for 30 minutes, stirring once in awhile. Add more water if chili appears too thick.
3. Serve with buns.

Yields: 6-8 servings

Spaghetti Meat Sauce

For rainy, dreary days when nothing but comfort food will do, here is a hearty and satisfying sauce.

1 lb.	ground beef	500 g
½ cup	chopped onions	125 mL
1-2	garlic cloves, minced	1-2
½ cup	chopped celery	125 mL
2 x 5½ oz.	cans tomato paste	2 x 156 mL
2 tbsp.	brown sugar	30 mL
¼ cup	vinegar	60 mL
2 cups	water	500 mL
1 tsp.	dry mustard	5 mL
2 tsp.	Worcestershire sauce	10 mL
1 tsp.	soy sauce	5 mL
	salt, pepper and chili powder to taste	

1. Brown the ground beef. Add onions and celery and simmer until vegetables are tender.
2. Add remaining ingredients and mix well.
3. Simmer for 1 hour. Add more water if sauce appears too thick.

Yields: 4 servings

Serve over hot spaghetti or your favorite pasta shapes.

Howling Coyote Meat Sauce

2 lbs.	ground beef	1 kg
1 cup	chopped celery	250 mL
1 cup	chopped green peppers	250 mL
1	large onion, diced	1
½ cup	prepared hot salsa*	125 mL
2 cups	tomato sauce	500 mL
¼ cup	apple cider vinegar	60 mL
3 tbsp.	Worcestershire sauce	45 mL
2 tbsp.	brown sugar	30 mL
1 tsp.	salt	5 mL
2	bay leaves	2
dash	cayenne pepper	dash
	Parmesan cheese	

1. In a large skillet, brown ground meat, celery, peppers and onion.
2. Add all other ingredients, except cheese, blend well, cover and simmer for 1 hour, stirring occasionally.**

Yields: 6-8 servings

Serve over spaghetti and sprinkle with Parmesan cheese. Marinated tomatoes and onions go well with this meal and Chianti wine adds a great accent. Cool Tropical Lime Cheesecake, page183, for dessert will "cool" your palate!

* For a little less "howl", use a milder salsa.
** This may also be cooked in a crock-pot for 7-8 hours on slow.

Meatloaf with Caper Sauce

Not your everyday meatloaf recipe, this is very tasty and moist with a rich, tangy sauce. As rangy-tangy as a Cowboy after round-up!

1½ lbs.	ground beef	750 g
½ cup	raw shredded carrots	125 mL
1 cup	shredded Cheddar cheese	250 mL
¾ cup	dry bread crumbs	175 mL
1	egg, slightly beaten	1
1½ tsp.	salt	7 mL
¼ tsp.	coarse pepper	1 mL
¼ tsp.	nutmeg	1 mL
1 tbsp.	prepared mustard	15 mL

Caper Sauce:

1¼ cup	beef stock	300 mL
3 tbsp.	capers*	45 mL
3 tbsp.	caper juice	45 mL
2 tbsp.	cornstarch	30 mL
3 tbsp.	water	45 mL
½ tsp.	sugar	2 mL
¼ cup	cereal OR whipping cream	60 mL
	salt and pepper to taste	

1. In a large bowl, mix all meatloaf ingredients and blend well. Pack into a 5 x 9" (13 x 23 cm) loaf pan. Brush with more mustard.
2. Bake at 350°F (180°C) for 1 hour. Let meatloaf stand and prepare sauce.
3. To make sauce, heat beef stock; add capers including juice. Simmer 3 minutes.
4. Combine cornstarch with water to make a thin paste. Add to stock; stir and cook until thickened.
5. Remove sauce from heat; add sugar and cream. Blend well. Return to heat; heat through, but do not boil.
6. Add salt and pepper to taste.
7. Slice meat loaf and spoon sauce over meat slices. Save some sauce for the noodles or potatoes.

Yields: 6-8 servings

Serve with either mashed potatoes or broad noodles. And don't forget a fresh mixed green salad.

* Capers are pickled flower buds from a bush found around the Mediterranean. Available in most supermarkets, they have a zesty, pungent flavor.

Old-Country Cabbage Rolls

These are not the small, rice-filled Ukrainian-style cabbage rolls. They are large, meat-filled rolls and the flavor is completely different, with a moist tomato-caraway sauce.

1	large head of cabbage	1

Beef Filling:

1 lb.	ground beef	454 g
1 cup	cooked rice	250 mL
1	large onion, chopped	1
1	egg, slightly beaten	1
1 tsp.	salt	5 mL
¼ tsp.	pepper	1 mL
3 tbsp.	ketchup	45 mL
1	garlic clove, minced	1

Tomato Caraway Sauce:

4 cups	tomato sauce	1 L
1 tsp.	caraway seeds	1 mL

1. Remove the thickest part of the cabbage core; boil cabbage in salted water for 10 minutes. Turn cabbage and cook another 10 minutes. Drain and let cool.
2. Cut out remaining cabbage core and separate leaves.
3. Combine all the ingredients for the filling. Blend thoroughly.
4. Place equal portions of meat mixture, about 4 oz. [115 g (⅓-½ cup)] in centers of leaves, fold ends over and roll up. Repeat with a second, larger leaf around the first rolled leaf.
5. Place rolls tightly together, rolled-up ends down, in a roasting pan.
6. Prick surface of cabbage rolls with a fork.
7. Pour tomato sauce evenly over cabbage rolls; sprinkle with caraway seeds; cover and bake at 325°F (160°C) for 1½ hours.

Yields: 6-8 servings

Serve with mashed potatoes.

Herbed Citrus Chops

This rather exciting combination of orange, Dijon mustard and rosemary turns an easy-to-make dish into a holiday affair! This dish is not just visually attractive, but also has a very pleasing aroma. And of course rosemary is known to promote the body's digestion of fatty meats.

Herbed Citrus Marinade:

1 cup	orange juice	250 mL
2 tbsp.	honey OR sweet and sour barbecue sauce	30 mL
1 tbsp.	Dijon prepared mustard	15 mL
2 tbsp.	chopped onion	30 mL
1 tsp.	crushed dried rosemary	5 mL
1	medium orange, well-washed	1
4	pork steaks	4

1. In an electric blender, blend juice, honey or barbecue sauce, mustard, onion and rosemary.
2. Grate peel from orange and add to marinade.
3. Place pork steaks in a large bowl or large sealable bag. Pour marinade over steaks. Cover dish or seal bag. Refrigerate for 1 hour.
4. Shake and turn bag or bowl occasionally.
5. Preheat barbecue or grill.
6. Remove steaks from marinade and pat dry with paper towels. Reserve marinade.
7. Barbecue over medium heat or broil in oven 4" (10 cm) from heat source, 5-7 minutes on each side. Brush steaks frequently with marinade.
8. Slice orange in thin slices and use to garnish steaks.

Yields: 4 servings

To round off this meal, serve with Cheese Tortellini in Famous Barrier Dill Sauce, page 82, and Company Cauliflower, page 106. For a tantalizing finale, serve Cappuccino Mocha Dessert, page 191.

Pictured opposite.

Wild West's Best (Pork)
Herbed Citrus Chops, page 156
Cauliflower Salad with Capers, page 71
Turnip Potatoes, page 102

Pork Chops and Sauerkraut

You will love this dish, the flavors are sweet and rich and it takes only 20 minutes to prepare.

6	pork chops	6
½ cup	sweet and sour barbecue sauce	125 mL
2 cups	well-drained sauerkraut	500 mL
½ cup	chopped onion	125 mL
½ cup	barley	125 mL
1 tsp.	caraway seed	5 mL
2 tbsp.	sugar	30 mL
½ cup	water	125 mL

1. Brush chops on both sides with barbecue sauce.
2. Combine sauerkraut, onion, barley, caraway seed, sugar and water in 2-quart (2 L) casserole.
3. Place pork chops over sauerkraut. Cover and bake at 325°F (160°C) for 1½ hours.

Yields: 6 servings

To serve, place sauerkraut in an oval serving dish and arrange pork chops on top. Embarrassingly simple and consistently delicious. Wonderful with mashed potatoes, and for dessert try the Raspberry Cream, page 191.

The mushroom pickers with their harvest,
see story on page 105.

Outdoor activities at
Barrier Chaparral Ranch.

Wild West's Best   159

Texas-Barbecued Pit-Style Ribs

8 lbs.	beef short ribs	3.5 kg

Texas Barbecue Sauce:

1½ cups	ketchup	375 mL
12 oz.	can beer OR non-alcoholic beer	375 mL
½ cup	cider vinegar	125 mL
½ cup	Worcestershire sauce	125 mL
1	onion, diced	1
5	garlic cloves, minced	5
¼ tsp.	hot pepper sauce	1 mL

1. Trim excess fat from ribs.
2. Stir all sauce ingredients together, pour over ribs and refrigerate overnight.
3. Spray grill rack with nonstick cooking spray. Preheat grill or barbecue.
4. Place ribs over medium heat, grill 45 minutes, turning every 15 minutes, brushing with sauce each time.

Yields: 8-10 servings

A real western meal, serve with Special Potato Salad, page 66, and Grilled Corn, page 108. End the meal with a slice of Chocolate Delight Pie, page 192.

FRIENDS . . .
enjoy the modern version of WESTERN FARE . . .
Here is what was said about the old one:

*Only a bucking bronco could stir a
man's innards enough to digest the tough*
WESTERN FARE.

*Saloon food was confined to the
"Basic Four B's"
Sourdough Biscuits
Beans
Beef
and Bacon (overland trout in cowboyese).*

Zesty Barbecued Pork Ribs

This meat dish is fast and easy, perfect for those hot summer days or as a welcome change in the midst of winter, when you can use the oven method.

2-3 lbs.	pork spareribs, cut into sections	1-1.5 kg
⅔ cup	vegetable oil	150 mL
½ cup	vinegar	125 mL
⅓ cup	sugar	75 mL
1 tsp.	Italian herb blend (basil, oregano, rosemary, thyme)	5 mL
½ tsp.	salt	2 mL
2	garlic cloves, minced	2

1. In a large saucepan, cook ribs in simmering water for 30 minutes; drain*.
2. In a large bowl, with a tight-fitting lid, combine oil, vinegar, sugar, herbs, salt and garlic; stir until sugar is dissolved. Add ribs, close lid, shake bowl well to cover ribs with the marinade.
3. Marinate 1-2 hours, shaking bowl occasionally. Do not refrigerate.
4. Preheat barbecue. Barbecue ribs over medium heat for 10-15 minutes, turning and basting with marinade frequently. This method keeps ribs moist and prevents barbecue flare-ups.

Yields: 4-6 servings

Serve with Baked Potatoes and Ranch Topping, page 80. A Crispy Carrot & Radish Salad, page 75, will complement this meal and as a crowning glory, serve Saskatoon Dumpling Dessert, page 178.

* The cooking water can be chilled, defatted and used as soup stock.

Wild West's Best

Honeyed Ham with Cloves & Mustard Gravy

| 2 lb. | whole ham | 1 kg |
| 1 tsp. | whole cloves | 5 mL |

Honey Mustard Glaze:

½ cup	brown sugar	125 mL
⅓ cup	lemon juice	75 mL
¼ cup	honey	60 mL
1 tsp.	dry mustard	5 mL

1. Press whole cloves into ham.
2. In a small saucepan, bring all glaze ingredients to a boil.
3. Baste ham with glaze.
4. Place ham in roasting pan and bake at 325°F (160°C) for 2 hours. Basting frequently during cooking.

Yields: 4-6 servings

Ham and Mustard Gravy, page 85, make excellent partners. Serve it with Sweet and Sour Red Cabbage, page 113.

Sweet Snacking

(Cookies & Cakes)

Ranch-Style Gingerbread Cookies with Pumpkin Dip

1 cup	butter OR margarine, softened	250 mL
2 cups	sugar	500 mL
2	eggs	2
½ cup	molasses	125 mL
4 cups	all-purpose flour	1 L
4 tsp.	baking soda	20 mL
2 tsp.	cinnamon	10 mL
1 tsp.	ground ginger	5 mL
1 tsp.	ground cloves	5 mL
1 tsp.	salt	5 mL
	additional sugar	

Pumpkin Dip:

8 oz.	light cream cheese, softened	250 mL
19 oz.	can pumpkin pie filling	540 mL
2 cups	icing sugar	500 mL
½-1 tsp.	cinnamon	2-5 mL
¼-½ tsp.	ground ginger	1-2 mL

1. In a mixing bowl, cream butter and sugar. Add eggs, 1 at a time, beating well. Add molasses, mix well.
2. Combine flour, baking soda, cinnamon, ginger, cloves and salt. Add to creamed mixture and mix well.
3. Chill overnight.
4. Preheat oven to 375°F (190°C).
5. Shape dough into 1" (2.5 cm) balls. Roll in sugar. Place 2" (5 cm) apart on ungreased cookie sheets.
6. Bake cookies for 6 minutes, or until edges begin to brown. Cool 2 minutes before removing from pan.
7. To prepare Pumpkin Dip, beat cream cheese in mixing bowl until smooth. Add pumpkin pie filling; beat well. Beat in sugar, cinnamon and ginger. Serve with the cookies.

Yields: approximately 18 dozen cookies; about 3 cups (750 mL) of dip

Store leftover dip in refrigerator. Enjoy!!!

Pictured on page 69.

Annie's Buttery Gingercake

This is an old Jewish recipe that found it's way to the "Wild West".

My friend Annie can tell her own version of an "Anne Frank" story. She lived in Holland hiding from the Nazis for 4 years before the Canadian Army liberated Holland. Annie came to Saskatchewan with her husband in the 50s and built up a very successful and thriving furniture business. Annie has the knack of making everybody feel good and warm and cared for, and that's exactly what this wonderfully rich cake does. When you feel lonely and uncared for . . . bake this Gingercake and indulge!

2 cups	butter	500 mL
1½ cups	sugar	375 mL
4 cups	flour	1 L
¾ cup	preserved ginger in syrup*, drained and finely chopped	175 mL

1. Preheat oven to 350°F (180°C) for 45 minutes.
2. Combine all ingredients well; knead until well blended.
3. Press into a well-greased 9 x 13" (23 x 33 cm) pan and bake for 45 minutes.
4. Cut in small squares.

Yields: 15-20 squares

Unforgettable!!

* Save the ginger syrup to sweeten tea or substitute as part of the liquid in a cake recipe to add a lovely ginger flavor.

Oatmeal Cake

Children and adults alike love this cake. Very much like a matrimonial slice, it's moist crumbly texture and rich date filling are perfect with afternoon tea or coffee.

1½ cups	quick cooking oatmeal	375 mL
1½ cups	boiling water	375 mL
2 cups	pitted, finely chopped dates	500 mL
1 cup	water	250 mL
1 cup	butter	250 mL
1 cup	brown sugar	250 mL
1 tsp.	vanilla	5 mL
1½ cups	all-purpose flour	375 mL
1½ tsp.	baking powder	7 mL
1½ tsp.	baking soda	7 mL
2	eggs, slightly beaten	2

1. Pour boiling water over oatmeal and let stand 15 minutes.
2. Cook dates in 1 cup (250 mL) water until mixture has a paste-like consistency. If too thick to spread, add more water.
3. Preheat oven to 325°F (160°C).
4. Cream butter, brown sugar and vanilla until creamy. Sift together flour, baking powder and baking soda.
5. Combine dry ingredients, creamed butter mixture, eggs and oatmeal. Mix lightly.
6. Spread half the dough into a greased 9 x 13" (23 x 33 cm) pan.
7. Spread date filling evenly over dough base.
8. Place remaining dough over date filling.
9. Bake for 1 hour.

Yields: 15-18 servings

Rhubarb Matrimonial Squares

Great for an afternoon coffee break, make this especially in spring when the rhubarb is plentiful. These squares freeze very well too.

3 cups	rhubarb	750 mL
1½ cups	sugar	375 mL
2 tbsp.	cornstarch	30 mL
1½ cups	flour	375 mL
¼ tsp.	baking soda	1 mL
1 cup	brown sugar	250 mL
1¾ cups	rolled oats	425 mL
¼ cup	butter	160 mL

1. Preheat oven to 375°F (190°C).
2. Cut rhubarb into ½" (1.3 cm) pieces. In a small saucepan, cook rhubarb with 1 cup (250 mL) of sugar until tender.
3. Combine ½ cup (125 mL) of sugar with cornstarch; stir into cooked rhubarb and continue cooking 4-5 minutes. Cool.
4. Sift flour with baking soda. Combine flour, brown sugar and rolled oats; cut in butter.
5. Pat half of oat mixture in well-oiled 9" (23 cm) square baking pan.
6. Spoon rhubarb filling over oat mixture; put other half of oat mixture on top.
7. Bake for 35-45 minutes. When cool cut into squares.

Yields: 12 servings

Rhubarb Cake

2 cups	all-purpose flour	500 mL
1 tsp.	baking soda	5 mL
½ tsp.	salt	2 mL
½ cup	softened butter, margarine OR vegetable oil	125 mL
1 cup	white sugar	250 mL
1	egg, beaten	1
1 tsp.	vanilla	5 mL
1 cup	sour milk*	250 mL
2 cups	chopped fresh rhubarb (do not use frozen rhubarb)	500 mL
1 tbsp.	sugar	15 mL
½ tsp.	cinnamon	2 mL

1. Preheat oven to 375°F (190°C).
2. Measure flour, baking soda and salt into flour sifter.
3. Beat butter or oil, sugar, egg and vanilla.
4. Add sifted flour to sugar mixture alternately with sour milk. Coat the rhubarb with some extra flour before you add it to the batter. This prevents it from settling in the bottom of the pan.
5. Pour batter into a 9 x 13" (23 x 33 cm) pan.
6. Combine 1 tbsp. (15 mL) sugar with cinnamon and sprinkle over the cake before putting it in the oven.
7. Bake for 40-50 minutes.

Yields: 15-18 servings

Double this recipe and it will make 3, 8" (20 cm) square pans.
It freezes well!

Variation: Make a delicious Apple Cake by substituting fresh apples for rhubarb.

* To make sour milk, put 1 tbsp. (15 mL) of vinegar or lemon juice in a cup and fill the cup with milk; let stand for 5 minutes.

Saskatoon Berry Cake

Another recipe with these wonderful berries that grow so abundantly in our area. A two-hour picking raid assures a pail of berries and an array of flavorful dishes. Every Indian tribe that lived in these regions cherished and used these berries for hundreds of years.

2 cups	all-purpose flour	500 mL
1 cup	sugar	250 mL
1 tsp.	baking powder	5 mL
1 cup	butter OR margarine, softened	250 mL
1	egg, slightly beaten	1
2-3 cups	Saskatoon berries, cleaned and rinsed	500-750 mL
2 tbsp.	lemon juice	30 mL
2 tbsp.	flour	30 mL
¼ cup	sugar	60 mL

1. Preheat oven to 350°F (180°C).
2. Combine flour, sugar and baking powder. Add butter and egg and combine until mixture resembles coarse crumbs.
3. Remove 1 cup (250 mL) of flour mixture for topping. Press remaining mixture into a 9 x 13" (23 x 33 cm) well-greased pan.
4. Spread berries over crumb base. Sprinkle with lemon juice.
5. Mix 2 tbsp. (30 mL) flour with ¼ cup (60 mL) sugar and sprinkle over berries.
6. Top with the remaining crumb mixture. Bake for 30-45 minutes.

Yields: 15 servings

Serve this cake warm with ice-cream.

Mom's Apple Cake

My mother who is now 88 years old made this cake throughout my childhood and as an especially "homey" treat when I came to visit her in later years. Only . . . my mother never, ever measured any ingredients. Her method was 3 fistfuls of flour, 1 good "grab" of butter, 3-4 shakes of cinnamon, nutmeg, salt and baking soda, 4 handfuls of apples, a sprinkling of nuts and a dribble of vanilla with a taste here and there, that made a beautiful Apple Cake. To this day; she makes it just that way and it always, always turns out perfectly. Would you like to try it that way? Go ahead but for the not so adventurous, try my version. It will turn out beautifully too!

3 tbsp.	butter OR margarine, softened	45 mL
1 cup	granulated sugar	250 mL
1	egg, beaten	1
1 cup	all-purpose flour	250 mL
½ tsp.	ground cinnamon	2 mL
½ tsp.	ground nutmeg	2 mL
½ tsp.	salt	2 mL
1 tsp.	baking soda	5 mL
3 cups	diced peeled apples	750 mL
¼ cup	chopped nuts	60 mL
1 tsp.	vanilla extract	5 mL

1. Preheat oven to 350°F (180°C).
2. In a mixing bowl, cream butter, sugar and egg. Stir together dry ingredients; add to creamed mixture. Batter will be very thick.
3. Stir in the apples, nuts and vanilla.
4. Spread batter in a greased 8" (20 cm) square baking pan.
5. Bake for 35-40 minutes, or until cake tester inserted into the center comes out clean, or center springs back when touched lightly.

Yields: about 9 servings

Serve warm or cold with whipped cream or ice cream.

German Apple Torte

This showy and elegant torte is a real hit every time we make it for our guests! It takes a little more effort than a plain apple cake, but it is well worth the time.

Crust:

½ cup	butter OR hard margarine (softened)	125 mL
⅓ cup	sugar	75 mL
1 cup	all-purpose flour	250 mL

Creamy Raspberry Filling:

½ cup	raspberry jam	125 mL
8 oz.	cream cheese, softened	250 g
¼ cup	sugar	60 mL
1	large egg	1
½ tsp.	vanilla	2 mL

Almond Apple Topping:

¼ cup	sliced almonds	60 mL
⅓ cup	sugar	75 mL
½ tsp.	cinnamon	2 mL
4 cups	thinly sliced peeled cooking apples	1 L

1. To make crust, cream butter and sugar together in a bowl. Mix in flour.
2. Press crust in bottom and halfway up sides of a 9" (23 cm) springform pan.
3. Spread jam over crust.
4. To complete the filling, beat cream cheese and sugar together.
5. Beat in egg and vanilla until blended, pour over jam.
6. Toast almonds in a 350°F (180°C) oven.
7. Preheat oven to 450°F (230°C).
8. To make topping, sift sugar and cinnamon together in a large bowl. Add apples. Toss to coat. Arrange over cheese mixture.
9. Sprinkle torte with toasted almonds. Bake for 10 minutes. Continue to bake for 25 minutes, or until apples are tender. Let stand at least 30 minutes before removing from pan.

Yields: 10-12 servings

Serve warm or room temperature. DO NOT FREEZE. Cut into 10-12 wedges.

Dream Cake

This cake is a "Dream", fast, easy . . . and with gourmet results. Dream on!!! Bake the cake a day or two ahead; it makes an unusual and wonderful birthday cake.

White Cake: Bake the cake a day ahead.

½ cup	shortening	125 mL
1 cup	milk	250 mL
1 tsp.	vanilla	5 mL
3	eggs	3
2¼ cups	all-purpose flour	550 mL
4 tsp.	baking powder	20 mL
½ tsp.	salt	2 mL
1½ cups	sugar	375 mL

Filling:

2 cups	blanched almonds*	500 mL
2 cups	whipping cream, whipped	500 mL
2 pkgs.	whipped cream stabilizer**	20 g
2 tsp.	almond extract	10 mL
⅓ cup	icing sugar	75 mL

1. Preheat oven to 350°F (180°C). Grease a tube pan and dust lightly with flour.
2. In a large bowl, combine shortening, milk, vanilla and eggs. With an electric mixer at low speed, beat for 1 minute.
3. Add the dry ingredients and beat for 2 additional minutes.
4. Pour batter into prepared pan and bake for 35-40 minutes, or until cake springs back when lightly touched. Cool 5 minutes, then remove from pan.
5. Place almonds on a cookie sheet and toast at 350°F (180°C) until golden brown, about 10-15 minutes. Let cool 5 minutes.
6. Using an electric blender, grind all but a few of the almonds as fine as possible. Keep 1 tbsp. (15 mL) of almonds for garnish.
7. Whip cream until stiff; add almond extract, icing sugar and the whipped cream stabilizer such as "Whip-It". Lightly fold in the ground almonds.
8. Cut cake twice horizontally; spread filling between layers and over the sides.
9. Press some whole almonds on the top for garnish.

Yields: 10-12 servings

* The success of this cake depends on the way the almonds are toasted and how finely they are ground.

** If stabilizer is not available, 2-3 tbsp. (30-45 mL) of cornstarch can be used instead.

172   *Sweet Snacking*

Drumstick Cake

This is for peanut lovers – indulge!

Peanut Base:

1½ cups	crushed vanilla wafers	375 mL
½ cup	chopped, unsalted peanuts	125 mL
¼ cup	butter OR margarine, melted	60 mL
2 tbsp.	peanut butter	30 mL

Creamy Peanut Butter Filling:

8 oz.	pkg. soft cream cheese	250 g
½ cup	sugar	125 mL
½ cup	peanut butter	125 mL
2 tsp.	vanilla	10 mL
4	eggs	4
4 cups	non-dairy whipped topping	1 L
½ cup	fudge sundae sauce (commercial)	125 mL

1. Preheat oven to 350°F (180°C).
2. To make base, mix together base ingredients. Save some for the top and press remainder into a 9 x 13" (23 x 33 cm) baking pan. Bake for 5-7 minutes.
3. To make filling, mix cream cheese, sugar and peanut butter in a large bowl.
4. Add vanilla and the eggs, 1 at a time, using an electric mixer on high speed.
5. Fold in whipped topping with a spatula.
6. Pour filling over base.
7. Drizzle fudge sundae sauce over the filling, and pull a knife through the fudge sauce to create a swirl pattern. Sprinkle with reserved crumbs and freeze.

Yields: 15 servings

Black Forest Cake

We can't call it a day at the ranch without a piece of this chocolatey temptation!!! This instant dessert is a great convenience on a busy day, try it when you need a chocolate treat in a hurry. It takes 10 minutes to prepare and the result is sensational. A must for young brides and cooks. It is always a success.

19 oz.	supermoist chocolate fudge cake mix	520 g
3	eggs	3
1 cup	chocolate chips	250 mL
19 oz.	can cherry pie filling	540 mL
2 tbsp.	almond flavoring	30 mL
2 tbsp.	amaretto	30 mL
	whipped cream for garnish	

1. Preheat oven to 300°F (140°C).
2. Ignore the cake mix instructions on the package and combine the above ingredients, except the whipped cream, very well.
3. Pour batter into a greased 9 x 13" (23 x 33 cm) baking pan and bake for 1 hour, or until cake springs back when lightly touched.
4. Decorate with whipped cream when cool.

Yields: 15-18 servings

This cake freezes very well.

Tantalizing Finales (Desserts)
Fresh Rhubarb Crisp, page 179
Saskatoon Dumplings Dessert, page 178

Tantalizing Finales

(Desserts)

Saskatoon Dumplings Dessert

We are so lucky to live at a place where Saskatoon berries are right at our front door. When it is berry-picking time all our guests very enthusiastically join in. These are always fun-filled days when mouths and hands are stained and big smiles greet the wonderful dessert at the end of the day. There are always requests to have it again and again and lots of offers to go and pick the needed berries.

4 cups	fresh Saskatoon berries OR blackberries*	1 L
1 cup	sugar, divided	250 mL
¾ tsp.	salt, divided	3 mL
½ tsp.	lemon extract	2 mL

Dumplings:

1½ cups	flour	375 mL
2 tsp.	baking powder	10 mL
¼ tsp.	nutmeg	1 mL
1 tbsp.	sugar	15 mL
⅔ cups	milk	150 mL
	cream OR whipped cream (optional)	

1. In a Dutch oven, combine the berries, 1 cup (250 mL) sugar, ¼ tsp. (1 mL) salt and lemon extract.
2. Bring to a boil; reduce heat and simmer for 5 minutes.
3. Meanwhile, in a mixing bowl, combine flour, baking powder, nutmeg, 1 tbsp. (15 mL) sugar and remaining salt.
4. Add milk and stir just until mixed. (Dough will be very thick.)
5. Drop dumpling batter by spoonfuls onto hot berry mixture; cover tightly and simmer until a toothpick inserted in a dumpling comes out clean, about 10 minutes.
6. Spoon into serving dishes. Serve with cream or whipped cream, if desired.

Yields: 8 servings

* Preserved Saskatoons, blueberries or canned blackberries may be used. Heat thoroughly and spoon dumpling mixture onto hot berries. Proceed to cook dumplings as above.

Pictured on page 175.

Photographs on page 176.

A Guest Cabin at Barrier Chaparral Ranch
Riders of all ages at the ranch

Fresh Rhubarb Crisp

Start making this with the first stalks in the garden or as an answer to the frozen packages in the freezer.

8 cups	diced rhubarb	2 L
1 cup	white sugar	250 mL
1 tbsp.	grated orange peel	15 mL
2 tbsp.	cornstarch	30 mL
⅓ cup	orange juice	75 mL
¾ cup	butter OR margarine	175 mL
2 cups	all-purpose flour	500 mL
1 cup	rolled oats	250 mL
¾ cup	packed brown sugar	175 mL
1 tsp.	cinnamon	5 mL
¾ cup	slivered almonds	175 mL
1	egg	1

1. In a 3-quart (3.5 L) casserole, toss the rhubarb with the white sugar and orange peel.
2. Dissolve the cornstarch in orange juice; add to rhubarb and toss to coat.
3. Preheat oven to 350°F (180°C).
4. Place the butter, flour, oats, brown sugar and cinnamon in a mixing bowl. Mix together until crumbly. Stir in almonds and mix in egg to bind the mixture.
5. Spread topping evenly over rhubarb. Bake until top is golden and rhubarb is bubbling, about 50 minutes.

Yields: 8-10 servings

Serve warm with ice cream or whipped cream!!

Pictured on page 175.

Apple & Banana Delight

This easy dessert will quickly become a family favorite. There are **no set quantities**; just use 1 small apple and half a banana per person. Make as much as you like.

apples
bananas
butter
brown sugar

Nutty Brown Sugar Crumble:

3 tbsp.	flour	45 mL
3 tbsp.	butter	45 mL
3 tbsp.	brown sugar	45 mL
2 tbsp.	chopped walnuts (optional)	30 mL

1. Peel, core and slice apples.
2. Peel and slice bananas.
3. Grease an 8 x 8" (20 x 20 cm) casserole or a size appropriate for the amount you want to make. Spread a 1" (2.5 cm) layer of bananas and apples in the dish.
4. Dot with butter and 1 tsp. (5 mL) brown sugar.
5. Repeat procedure until all the fruit you intend to use is used up.
6. Combine the flour, butter, brown sugar and chopped walnuts, if using, to make a crumbly mixture. Sprinkle over final layer of fruit.
7. Bake at 325°F (160°C) for 1 hour.

Yields: 9 servings for an 8" (20 cm) square pan. Double the Nutty Brown Sugar Crumble if you use a larger pan.

Serve warm with vanilla ice cream or whipped cream.

Creamy Rice Pudding

This very creamy stove-top rice pudding can be made a day ahead. Our guests say this is the best rice pudding they have ever eaten; I hope you agree with them.

2 cups	milk	500 mL
1 cup	cooked rice	250 mL
2 tbsp.	cornstarch	30 mL
2	eggs, beaten	2
⅓ cup	sugar	75 mL
1 tbsp.	vanilla	15 mL
1 tsp.	cinnamon	5 mL
½ cup	raisins, soaked in hot water	125 mL

1. Bring 1¾ cups (425 mL) of milk to a boil. Stir cornstarch into remaining ¼ cup (60 mL) cold milk, mix well and pour into boiling milk. Cook and stir over medium heat until quite thick.
2. Add a bit of the hot milk mixture to the beaten eggs; mix well and add a bit more of the hot milk mixture. Stir the egg mixture quickly into the milk mixture. Cook for about 2 minutes, but do not boil, stirring continuously.
3. Remove the pudding from the heat; add sugar, vanilla and cinnamon. Mix well.
4. Add cooked rice and drained raisins, blend well. Refrigerate until ready to serve.

Yields: 6 servings

This pudding can be served warm or cold.
Any leftovers can be refrigerated overnight.

Peach Kuchen

This dessert is not too sweet and you can use virtually any of your favorite fruits, including fresh fruits in season.

Crust:

1 cup	all-purpose flour	250 mL
¼ cup	sugar	60 mL
¼ tsp.	salt	1 mL
½ cup	butter OR margarine	125 mL

Sour Cream Peach Filling:

2 cups	sliced peaches OR a 19 oz. (540 mL) can of sliced peaches drained	500 mL
2	eggs	2
1 cup	sugar	250 mL
¼ tsp.	salt	1 mL
3 tbsp.	all-purpose flour	45 mL
1 cup	sour cream	250 mL

1. To make the crust, in a small bowl, combine flour, sugar and salt. Cut in butter to form a crumbly dough.
2. Pat dough lightly into an ungreased 8" (20 cm) square baking pan.
3. Preheat oven to 450°F (230°C).
4. Arrange peach slices over the crust; set aside.
5. In another bowl, beat eggs. Whisk in sugar, salt, flour and sour cream, until mixture is smooth.
6. Pour the sour cream over the peaches. Bake for 10 minutes. Reduce heat to 325°F (160°C) bake for 35 minutes more, or until center is set.

Yields: 6-9 servings

   Serve warm or chilled. Store in the refrigerator. This freezes well.

Pictured on page 69.

Cool Tropical Lime Cheesecake

In our sometimes very cool climate you need a "tropical" dessert once in a while to make you believe in summer and sunshine, beaches and suntans.

1¼ cups	macaroon cookie crumbs (about 10 cookies)	300 mL
¼ cup	butter OR margarine, melted	60 mL
1 cup	sugar	250 mL
3 tbsp.	cornstarch	45 mL
½ cup	water	125 mL
1-2 tsp.	grated lime peel	5-10 mL
⅓ cup	lime juice	75 mL
2	egg yolks, slightly beaten	2
16 oz.	cream cheese	500 g
1	drop green food color	1
½ cup	whipping (heavy) cream	125 mL

1. Combine cookie crumbs and butter thoroughly.
2. In an ungreased 9" (23 cm) springform pan, press crumb mixture firmly over the bottom. Refrigerate while preparing filling.
3. In a medium saucepan, mix sugar and cornstarch. Stir in water, lime peel and lime juice.
4. Cook over medium heat, stirring constantly until mixture thickens and boils. Gradually stir about ¼ cup (60 mL) of the hot mixture into egg yolks; stir back into hot mixture in saucepan.
5. Heat lime mixture to boiling. Boil and stir 1 minute; remove from heat.
6. Coarsely chop cream cheese and stir in with food color until cream cheese is melted and mixture is smooth. Press plastic wrap directly on the surface of the lime mixture. Refrigerate 30 minutes, or until cool.
7. Beat whipping cream until soft peaks form.
8. Fold whipped cream into the lime mixture; pour over crust.
9. Cover cheesecake and freeze until firm.
10. To serve, run a metal spatula along the side of the cheesecake to loosen; remove the sides of the pan.
11. Garnish with lime slices or twists and whipped cream if you wish. Let cheesecake stand 15 minutes at room temperature before cutting.

Yields: 8-10 servings

Pineapple Cream Pie

This unusual combination of coconut and pineapple is a favorite dessert for any occasion.

Coconut Pie Shell:

2 tbsp.	butter OR margarine	30 mL
1½ cups	flaked coconut	375 mL

Pineapple Cream Filling:

3 oz.	pkg. lemon gelatin	8.5 g
6 oz.	pkg. vanilla tapioca pudding mix	170 g
1¼ cups	milk	300 mL
10 oz.	can crushed pineapple, drained, juice reserved	284 mL
2 cups	whipped topping, non-dairy whipped topping OR whipped cream	500 mL

1. To make the pie shell, melt butter and stir in coconut; mix well.
2. Press coconut mixture into a 9" (23 cm) pie plate and bake at 300°F (150°C) for 15-20 minutes, or until crispy.
3. To make the filling, in a large saucepan combine lemon gelatin, pudding mix and milk; heat to boiling. Remove from heat.
4. Add ⅓ cup (75 mL) of the pineapple juice to the pudding mixture.
5. Cover filling with plastic wrap to prevent a skin forming. Chill until partially set.
6. Fold whipped topping into pudding mixture, add pineapple. Pour the filling into the coconut crust and chill 5-6 hours.

Yields: 8 servings

Sex-is-Best-in-the-West Dessert

You've never tried it? Please do. You will be hooked on it forever . . . the dessert that is . . .

1st layer:

1½ cups	all-purpose flour	375 mL
1 cup	chopped pecans	250 mL
¾ cup	butter OR margarine	175 mL

2nd layer:

8 oz.	cream cheese	250 g
½ cup	icing sugar	125 mL
4 cups	non-dairy whipped topping	1 L

3rd layer:

2 cups	milk	500 mL
4 oz.	pkg. vanilla instant pudding mix	106 g
4 oz.	pkg. chocolate instant pudding mix	106 g

4th layer:

4 cups	non-dairy whipped topping	1 L
	chopped pecans	

1. Mix ingredients for the 1st layer well and spread in a 9 x 13" (23 x 33 cm) pan. Bake at 350°F (180°C) for 15-20 minutes. Let cool.
2. Combine the 2nd layer ingredients and spread over the first layer. Let stand 5 minutes.
3. Combine the 3rd layer ingredients and spread over the second layer. Let stand 5 minutes.
4. Spread the topping on the 3rd layer and sprinkle with chopped pecans.

Yields: 25-30 servings

This freezes very well. I often use 2, 8" (20 cm) square pans, to make dessert for 2 meals.

Sinful Banana Pudding

Whenever I make this dessert, almost everybody asks for seconds. We have even had guests bidding at the table for the last remains in the bowl. An unbelievably popular dessert. I have given out his recipe to almost every guest – hundreds of them – and I am sure half of Europe is now indulging in Sinful Bananas. I must say this is the favorite dessert at the Ranch.

10½ oz.	can sweetened condensed milk (NOT evaporated milk)	300 mL
1½ cups	cold water	375 mL
4 oz.	pkg. vanilla instant pudding mix	106 g
2 cups	whipping cream, whipped	500 mL
36	vanilla wafers	36
3	medium bananas, sliced and dipped in lemon juice	3

1. In a large bowl, combine sweetened condensed milk and water. Add pudding mix; beat well. Chill 5 minutes.
2. Fold whipped cream into pudding mixture.
3. Into a large attractive glass bowl, spoon 1 cup (250 mL) of pudding mixture, top with ⅓ each of the wafers, bananas and pudding.
4. Repeat layering twice, ending with pudding.
5. Chill pudding until ready to serve.
6. Garnish as desired. Refrigerate leftovers, if there are any!!

Yields: 6-8 servings

Pumpkin Whip

A perfect alternative for pumpkin pie, if you love the taste of this autumn delight but object to the fat and calorie contents of the pie crust, then Pumpkin Whip is for you.

4 oz.	pkg. instant butterscotch pudding mix	106 g
1½ cups	cold milk	375 mL
1 cup	canned pumpkin	250 mL
1 tsp.	pumpkin pie spice	5 mL
1½ cups	non-dairy whipped topping	375 mL
	gingersnaps (optional)	

1. In a large bowl, beat pudding and milk until well blended, about 1-2 minutes.
2. Blend in pumpkin and pie spices. Fold in whipped topping.
3. Spoon into dessert dishes.
4. Chill and garnish with gingersnaps, if desired.

Yields: 6 servings

Yogurt-Quark Crème

A light and delicious summer dessert.

2 cups	unflavored yogurt	500 mL
1 cup	quark*	250 mL
1 tbsp.	lemon juice	15 mL
¾-1 cup	sugar	175-250 mL
1 cup	whipping cream, whipped	250 mL
½ cup	commercial chocolate fudge sundae sauce	125 mL
4 tbsp.	pistachio nuts, chopped	60 mL

1. Combine yogurt, quark, lemon juice and sugar in a large bowl. Blend with an electric mixer at medium speed. Gently fold whipped cream into quark-yogurt mixture. Refrigerate 3-4 hours.
2. When ready to serve, pour yogurt mixture into dessert dishes, drop 1 tsp. (5 mL) chocolate fudge sauce into the middle of each serving. Dip the tip of a teaspoon into the center of the fudge and pull outward, making a star-like design.
3. Sprinkle with pistachio nuts.

Yields: 6-8 servings

* Quark may be replaced with creamed cottage cheese blended until smooth.

Recipe for happiness

Take a cup of kindness
Add a dash of charity,
Mix with understanding
And a bit of courtesy,
Top it off with patience,
Sprinkle liberally with cheer –
Serve generously to everyone
you meet throughout the year!

Swedish Crème

This thick creamy dessert, a great finale to any hearty meal, looks spectacular with the red berries on top.

2 cups	whipping cream	500 mL
1 cup	sugar	250 mL
1 tbsp.	unflavored gelatin (1 env. – 7 g)	15 mL
1 tsp.	clear vanilla extract	5 mL
1 tsp.	almond extract	5 mL
2 cups	sour cream	500 mL
1 cup	crushed, fresh OR frozen raspberries	250 mL
2 tsp.	sugar	10 mL

1. In a saucepan, combine cream and 1 cup (250 mL) sugar.
2. Cook and stir constantly over low heat until steam rises from pan (do not boil).
3. Stir in gelatin until dissolved; add extracts.
4. Cool the cream mixture for 10 minutes. Whisk in sour cream.
5. Pour crême into 8 dessert glasses or small bowls; chill at least 1 hour. Before serving, combine raspberries and 2 tsp. (10 mL) sugar; spoon over each serving.

Yields: 8 servings

Variation: This dessert can also be poured into a large mold or individual molds. To serve, unmold on dessert plates and garnish with sweetened raspberries

Berries in Vanilla Custard Sauce

So good . . . So easy . . . So tasty!!!

Vanilla Custard Sauce:

1 cup	milk	250 mL
1	egg, slightly beaten	1
3 tbsp.	sugar	45 mL
1 tbsp.	cornstarch	15 mL
2 tbsp.	cold milk	30 mL
pinch	salt	pinch
½ tsp.	vanilla extract	2 mL
3 cups	fresh blueberries, raspberries or strawberries	750 mL

Berries in Vanilla Custard Sauce continued

1. In a saucepan, scald the milk. Combine egg and sugar in a bowl, stir in a small amount of hot milk.
2. Add egg mixture to the saucepan. Cook over low heat, stirring constantly. Add cornstarch dissolved in 2 tbsp. (30 mL) of cold milk. Heat and stir until mixture thickens slightly and coats a spoon, about 15 minutes.
3. Remove from heat; stir in salt and vanilla. Chill at least 1 hour.
4. Serve over berries.

Yields: 6 servings

Yogurt Strawberry Dessert

This is a fantastic dessert, heaven-sent for the diet-conscious. Showy, simple and unusual. One of my guests sent the recipe to me from Germany and it has been one of our favorites ever since.

1 lb.	strawberries, hulled and washed	500 g
2 tbsp.	lemon juice	30 mL
½ cup	sugar	125 mL
1 tbsp.	gelatin (1 env. – 7 g)	15 mL
¼ cup	orange juice	60 mL
1 cup	low-fat plain yogurt	250 mL
1 cup	crispy rice cereal	250 mL

1. In an electric blender, blend ½ the strawberries with lemon juice and sugar.
2. Soften gelatin in orange juice, heat and dissolve completely. Fold into strawberry purée and chill until partially set.
3. Cut remaining strawberries into small pieces.
4. Combine strawberry purée, strawberries and yogurt, stir gently. Stir in ⅓ cup (75 mL) of rice crispies.
5. Butter a 9" (23 cm) square glass pan, sprinkle with half of the remaining rice cereal. Pour strawberry mixture into pan. Sprinkle remaining cereal over berry mixture; press lightly into purée.
6. Refrigerate for 4 hours.

Yields: 6-8 servings

Strawberry Trifle

Sparkling in a glass bowel, this trifle version is a light and refreshing finale to a summer meal.

Jelled Layer:

4 cups	cubed pound cake	1 L
3 tbsp.	amaretto OR almond liqueur	45 mL
2 cups	sliced strawberries	500 mL
3 oz.	pkg. strawberry gelatin powder	85 g

Custard Sauce:

4 tbsp.	custard powder	60 mL
3 tbsp.	sugar	45 mL
2½ cups	milk	625 mL
3 tbsp.	amaretto	45 mL
1 qt.	non-dairy whipped topping, thawed	1 L

1. Place cake cubes in a 10-cup (2.5 L) glass serving bowl. Sprinkle with the amaretto. Add strawberries.
2. Prepare gelatin powder according to "quick set method" on package. Spoon slightly thickened gelatin over fruit. Chill until set.
3. Combine all custard sauce ingredients in a small saucepan. Cook and stir over medium heat until mixture comes to a full boil.
4. Place plastic wrap on the custard surface and chill for 40 minutes.
5. Stir amaretto into the custard and fold in 1 cup (250 mL) of the whipped topping. Spoon over set gelatin in bowl.
6. Let chill at least 2 hours.
7. Garnish with remaining whipped topping and some additional strawberries.

Yields: 10-12 servings

Raspberry Cream

UMMM heavenly!

1½ cups	frozen raspberries, thawed	375 mL
2 cups	mini-marshmallows	500 mL
½ cup	whipping cream, whipped	125 mL
3 oz.	pkg. raspberry gelatin	85 g
2 cups	sponge cake cubes	500 mL

1. Drain raspberries, reserving syrup.
2. Prepare gelatin according to package direction. Use the berry juice to replace part of the required fluid.
3. Add 1 cup (250 mL) mini-marshmallows to hot gelatin mixture; stir to partially dissolve them.
4. Chill until almost thickened. Whip until foamy. Gently fold in whipped cream, raspberries, cake cubes and the remaining mini-marshmallows.
5. Pour into an oiled mold, chill at least 4 hours. Unmold to serve.

Yields: 6-8 servings

Cappuccino Mocha Dessert

This luxurious light dessert, a favorite with our guests, is excellent after a heavy meal.

6	eggs, separated	6
¾ cup	sugar	175 mL
16 oz.	cream cheese, softened	500 g
⅓ cup	coffee-flavored liqueur, such as Kahlúa OR Tia Maria	75 mL
2 x ½ oz.	pkgs. commercial cappuccino mix	2 x 16 g
2 tbsp.	unsweetened cocoa powder	30 mL
8 oz.	pkg. vanilla wafers	250 g
8-10	whole coffee beans	8-10

1. Beat egg whites until soft peaks form, set aside. With an electric mixer, beat together egg yolks and sugar until thick and lemon colored. Add cream cheese, liqueur and the cappuccino mix; beat until thick and smooth. Fold egg whites gently into cheese mixture.
2. Cover the bottom of a large attractive bowl with about ½" (1.3 cm) of cheese mixture; sprinkle lightly with cocoa powder and press vanilla wafers in a single layer on top. Repeat procedure.
3. Lightly place a paper lace doily on top of the dessert, sprinkle ever so lightly with cocoa powder, lift off doily and finish decorating with wafers and coffee beans. Refrigerate 6-8 hours or overnight.

Yields: 8-10 servings

Chocolate Delight Pie

A heavenly combination; best of all it can be made ahead and keeps in the freezer for months.

Chocolate Wafer Crumb Crust:

⅓ cups	butter OR margarine	75 mL
1⅓ cups	crumbs	325 mL
¼ cup	sugar	60 mL

Creamy Chocolate Filling:

8 oz.	sweet chocolate (8 squares)	227 g
½ cup	milk	125 mL
8 oz.	cream cheese	227 g
4 cups	non-dairy whipped topping	1 L

1. In a small saucepan, melt butter, stir in crumbs and sugar.
2. Press the crumbs into the bottom and sides of a 9" (23 cm) pie plate.
3. Bake at 375°F (190°C) for 8 minutes. Cool before filling.
4. Heat 5 squares of chocolate with 1/4 cup (60 mL) milk in a large microwaveable bowl in a microwave on high for 11/2-2 minutes. Stir until completely melted.
5. Alternately, heat the chocolate in a heavy saucepan over very low heat. Stir until completely melted.
6. Beat in cream cheese and remaining milk.
7. Gently stir in whipped topping until smooth.
8. Spoon chocolate mixture into the crust; freeze until firm.
9. Remove from freezer. Let stand 30 minutes at room temperature, until pie can be cut easily.
10. Melt the remaining 3 squares of chocolate for about 15 seconds in the microwave; drizzle the chocolate over the pie.

Yields: 8 servings

Chocolate Lovers' Dream Dessert

No matter how long the trail, mention this dessert and everybody will be on time!

1 qt.	chocolate ice cream	2 L
1 cup	all-purpose flour	250 mL
¼ cup	quick rolled oats	60 mL
¼ cup	brown sugar	60 mL
½ cup	butter	125 mL
½ cup	chopped almonds	125 mL
1 tbsp.	cocoa powder	15 mL
1 cup	commercial chocolate fudge sundae sauce	250 mL

1. Let ice cream sit at room temperature while you prepare the crumbs so it softens enough to be spreadable.
2. Combine flour, rolled oats, sugar, butter, almonds and cocoa. Pat into a rimmed cookie sheet. Bake at 400°F (200°C) for 15 minutes, stirring occasionally.
3. Crumble baked crust while still warm. Cool.
4. Spread ¾ of the crumb mixture in a 9" (23 cm) square pan. Drizzle ½ of the chocolate topping over the crumbs. Cover with the ice cream. Drizzle with the remaining sauce and cover with the remaining crumb mixture. Cover and store in the freezer.

Yields: 6-8 servings

This will keep in the freezer for 2 months. A fantastic "make ahead" for those unexpected guests.

Thank you for the food we eat . . .

For those who share or serve it . . .

And if there be a good dessert . . .

Grace us to deserve it . . .

Rancho Cruncho Ice Cream Dessert

This crunchy caramel-flavored treat tastes especially wonderful after a long summer ride over the hot prairie.

8 cups	vanilla ice cream	2 L
1¾ cups	all-purpose flour	425 mL
1 cup	brown sugar	250 mL
1 cup	chopped pecans	250 mL
1 cup	rolled oats	250 mL
1 cup	melted butter OR margarine	250 mL
1½ cups	commercial chocolate fudge sundae sauce	375 mL

1. Let ice cream sit at room temperature while you prepare the crumbs so it softens enough to be spreadable.
2. Mix flour, brown sugar, pecans and rolled oats in a large bowl. Add melted butter and mix well.
3. Put in a thin layer on large cookie sheet and bake at 400°F (200°C), stirring occasionally, for 15 minutes, or until brown; crumble while warm, cool.
4. Press half of crumb mixture into a 9 x 13" (23 x 33 cm) pan. Drizzle with half the sauce. Spread with ice cream and the remainder of the crumb mixture and sauce.
5. Cover and store in the freezer.

Yields: 10-12 servings

Black Forest Ice Cream Dessert

This dessert will become everybody's favorite – it can be made ahead, ready to use anytime. Easy to make, it can be served in small or large portions and is elegant enough for company and absolutely delectable to eat.

8 cups	cherry ice cream	2 L
1¾ cups	all-purpose flour	425 mL
1 cup	sugar	250 mL
1 cup	toasted, chopped almonds	250 mL
1 cup	rolled oats	250 mL
1 cup	melted butter OR margarine	250 mL
1 tsp.	almond flavoring	5 mL
1½ cups	commercial chocolate fudge sundae sauce	375 mL
½ cup	maraschino cherries, chopped	125 mL
3 x 1 oz.	squares semisweet baking chocolate crushed into small pieces (do not replace with chocolate chips)	3 x 30 g
1 cup	whipping cream, whipped	250 mL

1. Let ice cream sit at room temperature while you prepare the crumbs so it softens enough to be spreadable.
2. Mix flour, sugar, almonds and rolled oats in a large bowl. Add melted butter and almond flavoring and mix well.
3. Spread in a thin layer on a large cookie sheet and bake at 400°F (200°C), stirring occasionally, for 15 minutes, or until golden brown. Crumble while warm. Cool.
4. Press half of crumb mixture into 9 x 13" (23 x 33 cm) pan. Drizzle with half the sauce, maraschino cherries and crushed baking chocolate.
5. Spoon whipped cream into ice cream until not quite combined; spread on crumb mixture.
6. Sprinkle remainder of crumbs and sauce over ice cream. Cover and store in freezer. It will keep well for up to 4 weeks.

Yields: 10-12 servings

Frozen Fruit Cups

This wonderfully light dessert is the perfect finale for a heavy meal, something small to satisfy that craving for a sweet to end the meal. Children love it as a snack. If you use low-fat yogurt, the fruit cups become a perfect diet dish.

3	bananas, very ripe	3
2 cups	peach OR orange yogurt	500 mL
1 cup	fresh OR frozen strawberries, thawed and undrained	250 mL
8 oz.	can crushed pineapple, undrained strawberries and/OR whipped cream for garnish	250 g

1. Mash bananas thoroughly. Add all other ingredients and stir gently.
2. Line 16-18 muffin cups with medium paper baking cups and spoon fruit mixture into cups. Freeze overnight.
3. Garnish with strawberries and/or whipped cream when serving. Let stand at room temperature for 15 minutes before serving.

Yields: 16-18 servings

These cups will keep in the freezer for 2 months.

Ranch Menus

Share the Spirit, Adventure and Romance of The West

Four-Week Menu Plan

This is the plan we follow at the Ranch. Many years of planning, testing and honing have gone into this. Our goal is to keep the meals balanced and easily digestible, tasty, easy to do and visually attractive. These menus get rave reviews from our ranch guests. Ignore the plan, follow it, or just have fun with it. The "Rise 'n' Shine" is your own preference. *Tip:* Do not follow a heavy breakfast with a large lunch.

Week 1

SUNDAY

Midday Roundup:
Supper:
Tantalizing Finale:

MONDAY

Midday Roundup:
Supper:
Tantalizing Finale:

TUESDAY

Midday Roundup:
Supper:
Tantalizing Finale:

WEDNESDAY

Midday Roundup:
Supper:

Tantalizing Finale:

THURSDAY

Midday Roundup:
Supper:
Tantalizing Finale:

FRIDAY

Midday Roundup:
Supper:
Tantalizing Finale:

SATURDAY

Midday Roundup:
Supper:
Tantalizing Finale:

Week 2

SUNDAY

Midday Roundup:
Oven French Toast 14
Supper:
Barbecued Steaks 147
Western Roundup Potatoes 102
Italian Vegetable Salad 78
Tantalizing Finale:
Ice Cream with Rhubarb Sauce 89

MONDAY

Midday Roundup
Grilled Ukrainian Sausage 124
Fresh Vegetable Platter with
Mustard Yogurt Dip 81
Indian Bannock 34
Supper:
Hill Dilly Chicken 145
Rice Loaf 103
Overnight Vegetable Salad 77
Tantalizing Finale:
Apple & Banana Delight 180

TUESDAY

Midday Roundup:
German-Style Fusilli Salad 46
Supper:
Bonanza Chili & Garlic Bread 151
Tantalizing Finale:
Cool Tropical Lime Cheesecake . . 183

WEDNESDAY

Midday Roundup:
Howdy Bean Soup 58
Supper:
Sauerbraten & Gravy 148
Mashed Potatoes
Baked Cabbage Wedges 112
Tantalizing Finale:
Swedish Crême 188

THURSDAY

Midday Roundup:
Trapper's Crispy Rice Pancakes 12
Creamy Coleslaw 74
Supper:
Corn-Muffin-Topped Buffalo Pie . . 119
Green Pea Salad 72
Tantalizing Finale:
Sinful Banana Pudding 186

FRIDAY

Midday Roundup:
Summer Luncheon Salad 42
Supper:
Catch of the Day à la Stroganoff . . 134
Rice
Marinated Carrot Salad 76
Tantalizing Finale:
Rancho Cruncho Ice Cream
Dessert 194

SATURDAY

Midday Roundup:
Gazpacho 64
Supper:
Herbed Citrus Chops 156
Company Cauliflower 106
Cheese Tortellini in Famous
Barrier Dill Sauce 82
Tantalizing Finale:
Cappuccino Mocha Dessert 191

SUNDAY

Midday Roundup:
Chicken Pita 48
Sliced Dill Pickles
Supper:
Barrier Buffalo Steaks 117
Broad Noodles
Calico Corn Salad 68
Tantalizing Finale:
Raspberry Cream 191

MONDAY

Midday Roundup:
Cauliflower or Broccoli
Cream Soup 63
Potato Biscuits 33
Supper:
Kicking Chicken Barbecue 144
Bacon & Egg Potato Salad 67
Cowboy Bean Casserole 111
Tantalizing Finale:
Black Forest Ice Cream Dessert . . 195

TUESDAY

Midday Roundup:
German-Style Fusilli Salad 46
Supper:
Old-Country Cabbage Rolls 155
Mashed Potatoes
Tantalizing Finale:
Yogurt Strawberry Dessert 189

WEDNESDAY

Midday Roundup:
Cordon Bleu Casserole 53
Supper:
Meatloaf with Caper Sauce 154
Fettuccini
Green Pea Salad 72

Tantalizing Finale:
Rhubarb Matrimonial Square 167

THURSDAY

Midday Roundup:
Settlers' Green Bean Soup 61
Supper:
Zesty Barbecued Pork Ribs 161
Baked Potatoes with Ranch
Topping 80
Crispy Carrot & Radish Salad 75
Tantalizing Finale:
Saskatoon Dumplings Dessert 178

FRIDAY

Midday Roundup:
Special Potato Salad 66
Barbecued Smokies
Supper:
Catch of the Day – in Aspic 136
Fried Potatoes
Yogurt Cucumber Salad 73
Tantalizing Finale:
Drumstick Cake 173

SATURDAY

Midday Roundup:
Roper's Blintzes 54
Supper:
Pork Chops & Sauerkraut 159
Garlic Potato Patties 101
Tantalizing Finale:
Orange-Kiwi Sauce 89

Week 4

SUNDAY

Midday Roundup:
  Terrific Tuna Salad 44
Supper:
  Grilled Buffalo Steaks 116
  Turnip Potatoes 102
  Overnight Vegetable Salad 77
Tantalizing Finale:
  Peach Kuchen 182

MONDAY

Midday Roundup:
  Grandma's Potato Soup 60
Supper:
  Spaghetti & Meat Sauce 152
  Cucumber Slaw 74
Tantalizing Finale:
  Pineapple Cream Pie 184

TUESDAY

Midday Roundup:
  Barbecued Shrimp & Scallop
    Kabobs 141
  Corny Ranger's Bread 38
Supper:
  Wild Goose Breasts à la Barrier
    Chaparral 129
  Stuffed Baked Potatoes 100
  Corny Casserole 108
Tantalizing Finale:
  Mom's Apple Cake 170

WEDNESDAY

Midday Roundup:
  Corn Chowder with Ham 62
Supper:
  Moose Balls with Tomato Sauce . . 120
  Broad Noodles
Tantalizing Finale:
  Chocolate Lovers' Dream Dessert   193

THURSDAY

Midday Roundup:
  Bacon & Egg Potato Salad 67
Supper:
  Venison or Beef Roast 123
  Mashed Potatoes
  Mushrooms & Sour Cream 104
Tantalizing Finale:
  White Cake topped with Rhubarb
    Sauce & Ice Cream 89

FRIDAY

Midday Roundup:
  Texas Chili Beans 152
  Mrs. Lindsay's Pioneer Buns 28
Supper:
  Salmon Barbecue 134
  Baked Potatoes
  Creamy Cauliflower Casserole . . . 106
Tantalizing Finale:
  Black Forest Cake 174

SATURDAY

Midday Roundup:
  Prairie Wheat Treat with Toast 15
Supper:
  Honeyed Ham with Gravy 162
  Sweet & Sour Red Cabbage 113
  Garlic Potato Patties 101
Tantalizing Finale:
  Frozen Fruit Cups 196

Index

SHARE *Horsing Around in the Kitchen* WITH A FRIEND

Order *Horsing Around in the Kitchen* at $19.95 per book plus $4.00 (total order) for shipping and handling.

Number of copies _____ x $19.95 = $ _____

Shipping and handling charge _____ = $ _____4.00_____

Subtotal _____ = $ _____

In Canada add 7% GST _____(Subtotal x .07) = $ _____

Total enclosed _____ = $ _____

U.S. and international orders payable in U.S. funds./ Price is subject to change.

NAME: _____

STREET: _____

CITY: _____ PROV./STATE _____

COUNTRY _____ POSTAL CODE/ZIP _____

Please make cheque or money order payable to:

Barrier Chaparral Western Vacation Ranch
P.O. Box 502
Tisdale, Saskatchewan   Canada   S0E 1T0

For fundraising or volume purchases, contact **Barrier Chaparral Western Vacation Ranch.**

Please allow 3-4 weeks for delivery

SHARE *Horsing Around in the Kitchen* WITH A FRIEND

Order *Horsing Around in the Kitchen* at $19.95 per book plus $4.00 (total order) for shipping and handling.

Number of copies _____ x $19.95 = $ _____

Shipping and handling charge _____ = $ _____4.00_____

Subtotal _____ = $ _____

In Canada add 7% GST _____(Subtotal x .07) = $ _____

Total enclosed _____ = $ _____

U.S. and international orders payable in U.S. funds./ Price is subject to change.

NAME: _____

STREET: _____

CITY: _____ PROV./STATE _____

COUNTRY _____ POSTAL CODE/ZIP _____

Please make cheque or money order payable to:

Barrier Chaparral Western Vacation Ranch
P.O. Box 502
Tisdale, Saskatchewan   Canada   S0E 1T0

For fundraising or volume purchases, contact **Barrier Chaparral Western Vacation Ranch.**

Please allow 3-4 weeks for delivery